Chess for Beginners

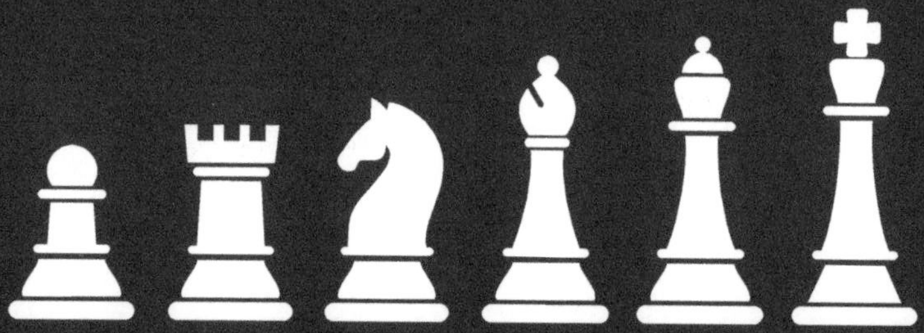

CHESS
FOR BEGINNERS

Know the Rules, Choose Your Strategy,
and Start Winning

Yelizaveta Orlova

ROCKRIDGE
PRESS

For general information on our other products and services or to obtain technical support, please contact our Customer Care Department within the United States at (866) 744-2665, or outside the United States at (510) 253-0500.

Rockridge Press publishes its books in a variety of electronic and print formats. Some content that appears in print may not be available in electronic books, and vice-versa.

Interior and Cover Designer: William D. Mack
Editor: Brian Hurley
Production Editor: Erum Khan

Illustrations © Conor Buckley, 2018

ISBN: Print 978-1-64152-257-1
eBook 978-1-64152-258-8

*Thank you to my
family and friends for
supporting me throughout
my chess career.*

CONTENTS

INTRODUCTION

My name is Yelizaveta Orlova, but call me Liza. I'm a Woman National Master and Woman Candidate Master, and these days I'm a full-time chess instructor living in Vancouver, Canada. You may have noticed that my name doesn't really look Canadian! I was born in Odessa, Ukraine, a beautiful city by the Black Sea. When it comes to chess, Ukraine is one of the top-ranked countries, both for the strength of its candidates and for the game's popularity—probably the reason most of my family knows how to play. I moved to Canada when I was three years old and started to play competitively by the time I was eight. My chess achievements include being the four-time Canadian Youth Chess Champion and the six-time Ontario Youth Chess Champion. I've also played twice for the Canadian Women's Chess Team.

My mother taught me the rules of chess when I was four years old. Once I began finding the game more difficult, however, I lost interest; only when I saw my father playing chess online almost every day did I take it up again, at the age of eight. Let me offer a piece of advice from my personal experience: If you have children, don't push them into a hobby; rather, pursue it yourself, and their interest will eventually develop on its own. I feel that seeing my father put so much effort into chess is what first got me intrigued. I kept thinking, "Why is my dad spending so much time on this cool-looking game?" My father was happy I got into the game, and he became my mentor—without his help, I wouldn't be the chess player I am today.

Today I teach private and semiprivate lessons, as well as group lessons at school lunch and after-school programs. I stopped playing competitively because I found it more enjoyable to share my knowledge with others. Playing for your country is a lot of hard work, and I'd like to pursue other hobbies in my spare time. I do know for sure that I will go back, but I have a few goals I'd like to achieve first. I founded a chess club in 2015 called Pub Chess Toronto, where people play in a social atmosphere. My goal is to get more people involved in chess, and they seem to like the noncompetitive atmosphere the social club provides.

Another activity I like to participate in is streaming chess on the online platform Twitch. When I stream on Twitch, people can see my chessboard and which moves I make. (I usually speak during the stream and explain why I am making the moves.) I also play against the viewers, who love seeing their game on the screen. I am so pleased about the opportunities that chess has given me outside of traditional playing—I feel like I don't have to work a day in my life, because I'm doing something I love.

Chess is an amazing game filled with an incredible number of possibilities. I am the type of person who gets bored with things that are too repetitive, so I found the nature of this game suited me perfectly—almost every game of chess you play is different.

The number of possible unique chess games is significantly greater than the number of electrons in the universe. The number of electrons is estimated to be about 10^{79}, while the number of unique chess games is 10^{120}.

As a child, I really grew to love this game because of the chess puzzles. If you're a fan of word or math problems, then I think you'll enjoy chess, too. You must think a certain number of moves ahead to achieve your goal. When you play the game, this is not so simple, since you must find the solution within the specific situation where a puzzle arises—chess is complicated. When I was little, I didn't like the memorization element of chess, which I found tedious, but all other aspects kept me wanting to play more and more!

Now that I'm older, I really believe that the game helps with academic studies and teaches life skills. Without chess, I wouldn't be the woman I have become. Chess taught me that you should never make a decision without thinking carefully about the ramifications.

For example:

- In chess, you must think prior to making a move, because it could potentially be a mistake.
- In life, you must think prior to speaking or acting, because there could be positive or negative consequences.

The game also teaches you about patience and both short-term and long-term goals. If you're not patient and you give up on future plans, you won't succeed. In life, we create short- and long-term goals alike: When we save money, we may envision a trip in the short term or a house in the long term. Regarding academics, chess uses the same part of the brain, educating your logical and strategic thinking.

Your level in chess doesn't matter; you will play at least a few beautiful games in your lifetime. Such a game usually requires sacrifice and the goal of winning in a small number of moves. You will see many examples in this book!

How to Use This Book

In this book, you will learn the rules of the game, basic tactics, and strategy. Once you have mastered the concepts in this book, I suggest you read more on specialized topics to continue improving your skills as a chess player. I will be demonstrating basic but occasionally complex situations, so once you've read the book the first time, go over it again, especially the diagrams.

Buying a chess set to try out the moves yourself would be a great asset. I am a strong chess player, but I still prefer to play out the moves on an actual chessboard, because while some players have photographic memory, others (like me) need to feel the moves with their fingertips. It's like when students memorize facts: Some students prefer to read over a topic multiple times to help them understand and remember, while others find they need to make notes.

To test you on key topics, you'll find quizzes throughout the book (most of them are not very difficult). At the end of the book, I also suggest websites where you can continue practicing chess puzzles on your own. In addition, I have included some fascinating facts about the game, and have even thrown in a few personal stories from the front lines of competition.

Enjoy!

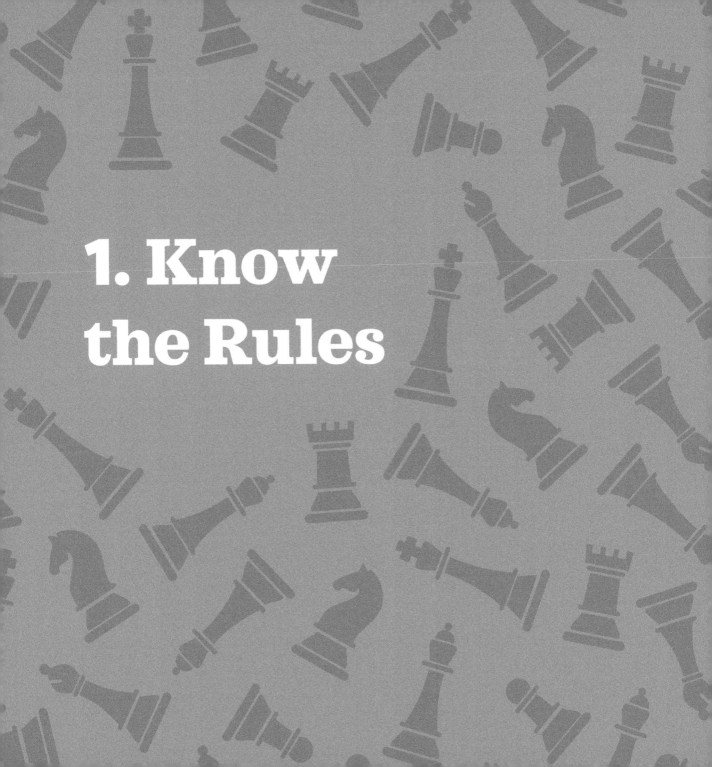

1. Know the Rules

A BRIEF HISTORY
of CHESS

Origins

Chess is one of the oldest board games of all time. It's believed to have been invented in India around 500 AD—about 1,500 years ago—but the game could potentially extend back even further. In the beginning, chess was known as *chaturanga*, meaning "four divisions (of the military): infantry, cavalry, elephantry, and chariotry." In approximately 600 AD, the game was introduced to Persia and the name changed to *chatrang*, which later became *shatranj*, due to its pronunciation. The words *check* and *checkmate* evolved from Persia, where "Shah!" means "King is under attack!" and "Shah Mat!" means "King is helpless!" Chess migrated from India to the Middle East, then on to Russia and Europe, at which point the game quickly gained popularity worldwide.

Throughout its history, chess has seen a number of changes. One of the first regards the starting position. In 500 AD, the Kings did not face one another, but in modern-day chess, they do. Before 1500 AD, the Queen and Bishop were weak, but their movement was changed so games wouldn't continue on for too long. Pawns used to be confined to moving one square on their first move, but this was changed around the same time as the establishment of another rule, called *en passant*. Castling, a special move in which you get your King to safety, was introduced around the fourteenth or fifteenth century but arrived at its current form by the seventeenth century. Chess has such a rich history, one could write a book on this subject alone!

Greatest Moments in Chess History

1. **TIMUR GAREYEV BREAKS GUINNESS WORLD RECORD:** Timur Gareyev, originally from Uzbekistan but currently living in and playing for the United States, broke the blindfold simultaneous exhibition (simul) record by playing 48 people at once—all while riding an exercise bike! Gareyev won 35 games, drew 7 games, and lost 6 games. The blindfold simul lasted about 19 hours and nine minutes. Even Magnus Carlsen (the number one chess player in the world) can't play as long!

2. **JUDIT POLGÁR:** Judit Polgár, originally from Hungary, is known to be the strongest female player of all time. Chess had never been very popular among women (the same problem occurs nowadays), yet Polgár was able to earn achievements of which only few can dream! Polgár earned the Grandmaster title in 1991 at the age of 15 years, four months—at the time, the youngest player in the world to achieve this. The first woman to surpass the 2700 rating, she grew as a player to become one of the top 10 in the world (among both women and men). Judit Polgár really made a difference in women's chess. A woman named Hou Yifan from China surpassed her rating in 2015, but so far, no one else has.

3. **GARRY KASPAROV AND DEEP BLUE:** Garry Kasparov is a renowned Chess Grandmaster and still holds the record as the youngest-ever World Champion of all time. He became World Champion at the age of 21 years, five months. Kasparov was challenged to play against Deep Blue, a supercomputer created by IBM. In the first match, in 1996, Kasparov managed to beat

the computer with a score of 4/6 (three wins, two draws, and one loss). A rematch was held the following year, in 1997, but Kasparov lost with the score of 2.5/6 (one win, three draws, two losses). It was still an amazing achievement for the chess community!

4. **MAGNUS CARLSEN ERA:** Magnus Carlsen, a Norwegian Grandmaster, is the current World Champion. Carlsen was a chess prodigy who earned the Grandmaster title at the age of 13 years, four months. At the age of approximately 22 (one or two weeks before his 22nd birthday), Carlsen became World Champion in 2013 by defeating the strongest Indian player, Vishy Anand. He was hoping to become the youngest World Champion but, sadly, was never able to beat the record of Garry Kasparov. Carlsen remains the World Champion and currently travels around the world playing chess. Carlsen has his own app where you can play him, called Play Magnus.

5. **BOBBY FISCHER, FIRST AMERICAN WORLD CHAMPION:** Robert James Fischer, better known as Bobby Fischer, was an American prodigy, a Chess Grandmaster, and the 11th World Champion. Fischer won the U.S. Chess Championship at age 14 in 1957, defeating the strongest players in the country. Years later, Bobby Fischer won the World Chess Championship against Russian player Boris Spassky. This was a huge milestone in chess history, considering that the United States and the Soviet Union weren't on the best of terms at that time. Sadly, Fischer isn't with us today; he died January 17, 2008, at the age of 64. Coincidentally, there are 64 squares on the chessboard.

Chess Today

TECHNOLOGY: Chess has changed a lot since the technology boom. Now, it's simple to learn the game by watching videos, reading articles, and exploring online chess platforms where you can play. You can also purchase books online on any chess topic. When it comes to being taught chess, thanks to the Internet, you can get an online coach, rather than trying to find a local chess instructor. If you're ever in need of extra help, you can use numerous chess sites to find the right fit for you, or you can find a coach in your local area. Back in the day, before computers and the Internet, it was harder to find chess material. If you wanted to play a game of chess, you'd have to go out and find it; there were no virtual options.

ACADEMICS: Chess is starting to become extremely popular among young school students. In North America, many schools offer extracurricular activities during lunch and after school hours. Chess has been known to help academic growth, which is why many parents introduce their children to the game. Armenia is one of the countries that include chess in their school curriculums. Sadly, only a few of these young masterminds will go into competitive play. If you love strategy games, puzzle solving, and mathematics problems, this game is certainly for you!

WORLDWIDE: Russia, Ukraine, and India have always been known to be the strongest chess countries in the world. The game itself is taken particularly seriously in those countries and is a popular pastime. The United States has become one of the strongest, as well, because many U.S. chess players have immigrated from other areas. Here's a chart showing the top 10 chess federations (as of June 2018):

COUNTRY RANK BY AVERAGE RATING OF TOP 10 PLAYERS

	Average Rating	Grandmasters	International Masters
1. Russia	2742	247	538
2. China	2709	45	34
3. United States of America	2701	96	152
4. Ukraine	2675	91	201
5. India	2673	51	99
6. Azerbaijan	2670	24	30
7. Hungary	2647	56	121
8. France	2647	51	108
9. Poland	2640	43	109
10. Armenia	2640	42	29

Source: FIDE–World Chess Federation, "Federations Ranking," June 28, 2018, http://ratings.fide.com/topfed.phtml.

Interestingly enough, the number one player today is from Norway.

Here are the top 10 chess players in the world:

TOP 10 CHESS PLAYERS

	Country	Rating	Birth Year
1. Carlsen, Magnus	NOR	2843	1990
2. Caruana, Fabiano	USA	2816	1992
3. Mamedyarov, Shakhriyar	AZE	2808	1985
4. Ding, Liren	CHN	2798	1992
5. Kramnik, Vladimir	RUS	2792	1975
6. Vachier-Lagrave, Maxime	FRA	2789	1990
7. Giri, Anish	NED	2782	1994
8. Karjakin, Sergey	RUS	2782	1990
9. So, Wesley	USA	2778	1993
10. Nakamura, Hikaru	USA	2769	1987

Source: FIDE–World Chess Federation, "Standard Top 100 Players September 2018," https://ratings.fide.com/top.phtml?list=men.

THE GOAL
&
THE BOARD

The Goal of the Game

The King is the most important piece whose status determines when the game comes to an end. The goal of the game is to get your opponent's King into a position where it is under attack, is unable to move, and cannot be helped by its own men; this is also known as *checkmate*. *Check* is when the King is under attack but can escape.

The important question: When the King is under attack, what can you or your opponent do?

The best way to remember is by using the ABCs.

THE ABCs OF CHECK

AWAY: Run away with the King to a square where it can't be captured.

BLOCK: Put a piece in between the attacker and the King.

CAPTURE: Capture the piece that is attacking the King.

An important rule to note is that the King can never be captured in chess. You are also not allowed to put your King into check (move on a square protected by an enemy player). Since this is an illegal move, if a person goes ahead and does this, he or she should take it back and make a legal move instead. It is also illegal to keep your King in check. When your King is under attack, you must stop all plans and protect your most important piece.

A player may also resign (give up) in a game by telling the opponent verbally, "I resign!" or by putting his or her King down.

But do all chess games end in a win or loss?

No! In fact, the game of chess allows for six different types of draws:

1. **AGREEMENT:** You may offer a draw to your opponent after you've made your move. If your opponent accepts, the game has come to an end. If your opponent declines, the game continues.

2. **INSUFFICIENT MATERIAL:** When both sides don't have enough pieces to checkmate either King, the game ends.

3. **50-MOVE RULE:** If a Pawn hasn't been moved or a piece hasn't been captured in 50 moves, either player may claim a draw. The only way to prove this scenario is to have the moves written down or an arbiter monitoring the game.

4. **STALEMATE:** When a player's King is not in check and no legal moves can be made, the game ends.

5. **PERPETUAL CHECK:** When a player checks the King repeatedly and is able to copy the exact same position three times, the game ends.

6. **THREE-TIME REPETITION:** Copying the exact position three times but without checks results in a draw.

Each of these draws will be covered more in depth in chapter 5.

The Board

The board consists of 64 squares on an 8-by-8 checkerboard. Half of the squares (32) are light, and the other half are dark. When you are placing the board in front of you, make sure the bottom right-hand corner is light. Just remember the helpful saying, "Light is on the right!" It doesn't matter whether you are playing White or Black, the right-hand corner square closest to you must always be light.

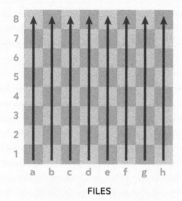

FILES

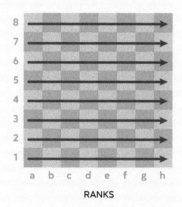

RANKS

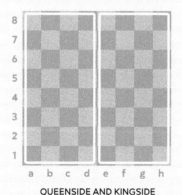

QUEENSIDE AND KINGSIDE

You might notice that there are letters and numbers along the sides of a chessboard; this is to provide each square on the board with its own name. We use these coordinates to write down our moves, but also to participate in chess conversations.

What is a chess conversation? If you're speaking to a friend or your chess instructor about a position, it is not correct to simply point at a square in discussing it; you must assign it a name. For example, you would say, "My Knight on c3 could have captured the Pawn on d5." There are also important terms we use, as well:

FILES are the vertical lines that divide the board into eight columns across. These include the a, b, c, d, e, f, g, and h files.

RANKS are the horizontal lines that divide the board into eight columns from bottom to top. These include the 1st, 2nd, 3rd, 4th, 5th, 6th, 7th, and 8th rank.

We can also divide the board in half vertically: **QUEENSIDE** and **KINGSIDE**. Queenside includes the a, b, c, and d files. Kingside includes the e, f, g, and h files. We might use one of these terms in a sentence, such as, "I castled my King on the queenside."

THE STARTING POSITION

Since White always moves first in chess, its pieces are located on the 1st and 2nd ranks; meanwhile, Black's pieces are placed on the 7th and 8th ranks.

There have been many explanations as to why White moves first. Personally, the one I like the most is that long ago, before glasses were invented, people preferred to play Black over White because it was easier to see the pieces. As a concession, those playing White could go first.

The **KING** and the **QUEEN** are royalty, so they are positioned in the center of the starting arrangement (d and e files). The King is the piece usually wearing a cross on its head (White's King: e1; Black's King: e8), while the Queen wears a tiara or crown (White's Queen: d1; Black's Queen: d8). Make sure to place the Queen on its own color!

ROOKS are the pieces that look like a tower of a castle. They are placed in the corners of the board, since the other pieces live "inside the castle."

KNIGHTS are the pieces that look like a horse. If we look back at medieval times, the high-ranked soldiers would fight on horseback. High-ranked soldiers lived inside the castle with the king, queen, and bishops.

KING AND QUEEN

ROOKS

KNIGHTS

BISHOPS

PAWNS

BISHOPS resemble popes in their attire and zucchetto (skullcap). Back in the day, when religion held a central place in society, Bishop was the common term used in chess. But today, there are many who are not believers— or are even atheists—so some chess instructors (including myself) call these pieces "Advisors of the King and Queen," as the real bishops would in fact help with any decision-making at the Round Table.

PAWNS are the pieces that look like a person without arms. Pawns were known to be low-ranked soldiers, which is why they guard the castle and everyone inside.

Voila! The starting position!

HOW *the* PIECES MOVE

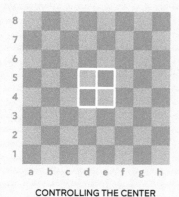

CONTROLLING THE CENTER

Before we go into how the pieces move, I want to make a point about controlling the center. Every piece in chess (with exception of the King) has a better advantage when placed toward the center. If you put your thumb in the center of the board, it will touch four squares: d4, d5, e4, and e5. Pieces have more mobility when they are closer to the center—if they are on the side of the board, on the other hand, they may have access to fewer than half of the squares.

I have included the value of pieces in this section because it's important to know their worth in relation to the others. This information allows you to decide when it is safe to capture a protected piece and when it isn't.

For example, should the Queen capture a protected Pawn? No, the Queen is worth 9 points and the Pawn is worth 1 point, so in capturing the pawn, you'd lose 8 points. Keep in mind that chess involves a little bit of math. I have also listed the tactical strengths of each piece—you will learn more about these tactics in chapter 7.

Pawn

WHITE: 8 **BLACK:** 8

MOVEMENT: One or two squares forward on the first move. Once a Pawn has moved, it continues only one square forward. Pawns never move backward.

CAPTURE: Diagonally one square forward

VALUE: 1 point

Why is the Pawn unique compared to any other piece?

1. Pawns move differently than how they capture. Every other piece moves and captures the same way.

2. Pawns can't move or capture backward.

3. If a Pawn gets to the other side of the board, it can transform into a piece other than the Pawn or King. (This is called **promotion** and will be covered in the next chapter.)

Pawns move forward but capture diagonally one square forward. The Pawn is the weakest in chess because of its relative lack of mobility—all other pieces can move or capture more than two squares. What is the reason why the Pawn can't move or capture backward? When I am in class, I tell students that since the Pawn is the low-ranked soldier, it is not allowed to return home until the battle is over.

PAWN MOVEMENT

PAWN CAPTURE

STRENGTHS

- Once a Pawn gets to the other side of the board, it can transform into a Queen, Rook, Bishop, or Knight
- Pawns are used to defend the King—wherever you decide to castle (we will cover **castling** in the next chapter), your Pawns should stay close by
- Tactical piece (fork)

WEAKNESSES

- Lack of mobility
- Can't move long distances
- Weakest piece in the game

STRATEGY

- At the start of the game, move your center Pawns first
- Once your King is castled, move your Pawns on the opposite side

Rook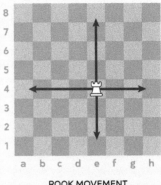

WHITE: 2 **BLACK:** 2

MOVEMENT: Vertical/Horizontal

CAPTURE: Vertical/Horizontal

VALUE: 5 points

Rooks move and capture horizontally (left/right) and vertically (up/down). Rooks can't jump over pieces and can get blocked by the opponent's pieces or those of their own color.

ROOK MOVEMENT

STRENGTHS

- A lot of mobility
- Can move long distances
- Control both light and dark squares
- Tactical piece (fork, pin, skewer, discovered attack, etc.)

WEAKNESSES

- Can't control diagonals

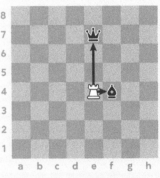

ROOK CAPTURE

STRATEGY

- Control open files
- Double up Rooks on an open file
- Get Rook(s) on the 7th or 8th rank (or 1st or 2nd if you're playing Black)

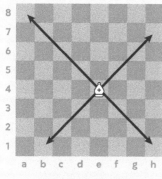

BISHOP MOVEMENT

Bishop

WHITE: 2 (one light square, one dark square)
BLACK: 2 (one light square, one dark square)
MOVEMENT: Diagonal
CAPTURE: Diagonal
VALUE: 3 points

Bishops move and capture diagonally on the chessboard. One Bishop controls only the light squares, while the other controls only the dark squares. Bishops can't jump over pieces and can get blocked by the opponent's pieces or those of their own color.

STRENGTHS

- A lot of mobility
- Can move long distances
- Control both light and dark squares
- Tactical piece (fork, pin, skewer, discovered attack, etc.)

WEAKNESSES

- Can't control files or ranks
- Can't control both dark and light squares if one Bishop has already been captured

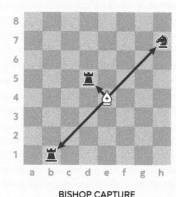

BISHOP CAPTURE

STRATEGY

- Control open diagonals
- Move in open positions, that is, positions with mostly open or semi-open files and diagonals
- Try to keep both Bishops

King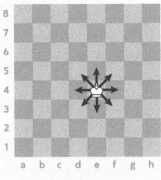

WHITE: 1 **BLACK:** 1
MOVEMENT: Vertical/Horizontal/Diagonal, only one square
CAPTURE: Vertical/Horizontal/Diagonal, only one square
VALUE: The game

The King is the most important piece and decides the game. It can move or capture in any direction, but only one square at a time. Remember: the King can *never* capture a protected piece—this would be an illegal move. You are also not allowed to put your King into check or keep it in check. Finally, the way to end the game is called checkmate.

Take a look at **DIAGRAM 3.1**. The King is under attack by the Rook on c6. Where can the King move, or what can it capture? The King can capture the Rook on b4 and the Pawn on d5.

Why can't the King move to other squares?

- Square b5: Protected by White's Rook on b4.
- Square b6: Protected by both of White's Rooks.
- Square c6: The Rook is protected by the Pawn on d5.
- Square d6: Protected by White's Rook on c6.
- Square d4: The Bishop is protected by the Rook on b4.
- Square c4: Protected by the Rook on c6.

STRENGTHS

- Controls both light and dark squares
- Tactical piece (fork)

KING MOVEMENT

KING CAPTURE

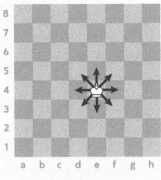

DIAGRAM 3.1

WEAKNESSES

- Lack of mobility
- Can't move long distances
- Constant target in the game

STRATEGY

- At the start of the game, hide the King on either the queenside or kingside (away from the center). Then, toward the end, bring the King out to play!

Queen ♛ ♕

WHITE: 1 **BLACK:** 1
MOVEMENT: Vertical/Horizontal/Diagonal
CAPTURE: Vertical/Horizontal/Diagonal
VALUE: 9 points

The Queen moves and captures in any direction, as far as it can on the chessboard. The Queen can't jump over pieces and can get blocked by the opponent's pieces or those of its own color.

STRENGTHS

- A lot of mobility
- Strongest piece in the game
- Controls both light and dark squares
- Tactical piece (fork, pin, skewer, discovered attack, etc.)

WEAKNESSES

- Doesn't really have any

STRATEGY

- Don't bring out the Queen too early, as it can be attacked or even trapped
- Bring the Queen out in the middle of the game, once the Knight and Bishops are developed
- Since the Queen is very powerful—the strongest attacker—try to include it in any attacks

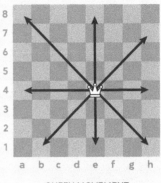

QUEEN MOVEMENT

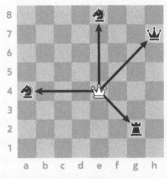

QUEEN CAPTURE

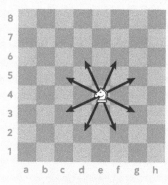

KNIGHT MOVEMENT

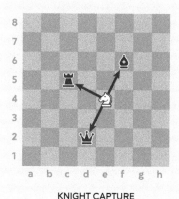

KNIGHT CAPTURE

Knight

WHITE: 2 **BLACK:** 2
MOVEMENT: *L* shape
CAPTURE: *L* shape
VALUE: 3 points

Knights move in an *L* shape, which means they can jump over pieces. Knights are the only pieces in chess that can jump and never be blocked! The *L*-shape move consists of three squares: either two squares horizontally followed by one square vertically, or two squares vertically followed by one square horizontally. When a Knight moves, it will always land on the opposite-colored square. For example, if the Knight sits on a light square, it will move to a dark square. Alternatively, if the Knight begins on a dark square, it will move to a light square.

STRENGTHS

- A lot of mobility
- Controls both light and dark squares
- Tactical piece (fork, discovered attack, etc.)

WEAKNESSES

- Can't control files or ranks
- Can't move long distances

STRATEGY

- Move in closed positions, that is, positions with mostly blocked files and diagonals
- Place a Knight on an outpost square (a square that can't be attacked by an enemy Pawn)

SPECIAL RULES

&

CHESS NOTATION

En Passant

En passant is a special move that originated in the fifteenth century when Pawns began moving two squares forward instead of one on their first move. When a Pawn advances two squares, it can jump over the square an enemy Pawn is protecting—many players probably regarded this as unfair.

To illustrate, here's a real-life war situation: A soldier (let's call him X) is waiting in place, pointing a gun at a certain area, while the enemy soldier (Y) knows his opponent's target. Is it possible for soldier Y to pass by without getting shot? Soldier Y can take the chance of running past soldier X, but it's really a gamble: He might get away with it, or he might get shot.

There's an important caveat behind this special move. If your opponent's Pawn moves two squares forward (cheating its own death), you can capture it, but *only* on that move. If you decline the en passant capture, you will not have a chance to capture the Pawn again—unless a new en passant situation arises.

As you can see in the diagram on the right, White's Pawn protects the c6 and e6 squares. Black moves their Pawn to e5, over the square White's protecting. White may or may not choose to capture the Pawn. Let's say they do. When capturing a Pawn with the en passant rule, you must capture it the way a Pawn captures, diagonally one square forward. It may look a bit strange, but Pawns do not capture horizontally.

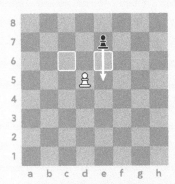

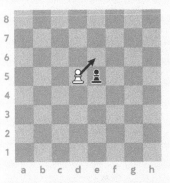

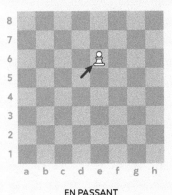

EN PASSANT

CHOOSING EN PASSANT

Should you always choose en passant? No! If your opponent doesn't know this rule and foolishly gave up a Pawn, sure. Otherwise, you must think strategically if the en passant capture is beneficial to your position. Take a look at the next example (on the left side of this page):

White's Pawn is yet again defending the c6 and e6 squares. Black moves to c5—going over the square White is defending. Should White capture the Pawn here? This depends on White's plan. If White wants to keep Black's pieces a little more passive, capturing en passant isn't the best idea, since this would allow Black to recapture the Pawn and develop their Knight. So what would be the benefit of capturing the Black Pawn? The d5 square would become free (unless Black captures with the Pawn instead of the Knight) for White's Knight to leap there. Chess is a complicated game! There are a lot of variables to consider.

Castling

The purpose of castling is to get your King to safety. As mentioned earlier, all pieces but the King have stronger positions in the center. Why would you want to leave your King where all the commotion is? Leaving the King there can place it in a lot of danger. The King is never 100 percent safe, but in drawing it away from the center, you can protect it with a fortress of Pawns standing guard. At the same time, castling can also help one of your Rooks advance toward the center of the board.

What makes castling a particularly interesting and unusual move? It is the only circumstance in which the King is allowed to move two squares and a Rook can jump over another piece (the King).

KINGSIDE CASTLE & QUEENSIDE CASTLE

Please note: It is extremely important that you move your King first, followed by your Rook. At a junior event, I touched my Rook first, so my opponent called the arbiter and forced me to move my Rook instead. Since then, I have always been particularly careful to move my King first. Luckily, I still won that game!

KINGSIDE CASTLE, BEFORE

KINGSIDE CASTLE, AFTER

QUEENSIDE CASTLE, BEFORE

QUEENSIDE CASTLE, AFTER

PIECES BETWEEN KING
AND ROOK

WHEN YOU'RE NOT ALLOWED TO CASTLE

Pieces Between the King and Rook

In the starting position, neither White nor Black can castle. If the King wants to castle queenside, it will have to move the Knight, Bishop, and Queen out of the way. If the King wants to castle kingside, it will have to move the Bishop and Knight out of the way.

King or Both Rooks Have Moved

If the King has moved, you'll have no chance to castle because there's only one King per side. If one Rook has moved, you will still be able to castle with the other. But don't think that moving your King or Rooks and then moving them back into the starting position will work. This is the reason you see most players castling in the first 10 moves in the game. The quicker you castle, the fewer obstacles will be in your way!

I'd like to tell you a story: In one of my first chess tournaments, I was supposed to write down the moves, but I accidentally didn't follow this rule and therefore didn't realize I had made a mistake. When I got home, I went over the game with my father, who said, "Liza, how could you have castled in this position? You already moved your King earlier in the game." Taken aback, I replied, "I think I'd forgotten I moved my King." "Well, you are very lucky that your opponent didn't notice this," he said. "I hope you have learned your lesson and won't make this mistake again. In chess, you have to follow the rules."

King Is in Check

In this scenario, Black is ready to castle the King, but White develops the Bishop with a check! You are not allowed to castle when you are in check—though I honestly have no idea why. Remember: If you move your King out of check here, you won't be able to castle for the rest of the game. On the other hand, if you block the attack, you can still castle on the following move!

KING IN CHECK

Going Through/Into Check

In this position, White is not able to castle on either the kingside or the queenside. Yet, neither side has pieces between the King and Rooks; the King is not in check, and the King and both Rooks have not yet moved—so what's the problem? There are, in fact, two. White can't castle queenside because Black's Rook is protecting the d1 square, so this would be going "through check." White also can't castle on the kingside because Black's Bishop is protecting the g1 square, so this would be going "into check."

GOING THROUGH/
INTO CHECK

PROMOTION, BEFORE

PROMOTION, AFTER

Promotion

Promotion is the ability of a Pawn to transform into a Queen, Rook, Bishop, or Knight when it reaches the other side of the board. Therefore, never underestimate the power of the Pawn! Ninety-nine percent of the time you will want to promote it to a Queen—but there are some rare exceptions.

What I've noticed throughout the years is that many kids are in a huge rush to get their Pawns to the other side, and they end up giving them away for free because they didn't think carefully enough before making a move. If you are thinking about promoting, make sure no enemy piece can capture you!

Chess Notation

Chess notation is the way we read or write moves in a chess game or diagram. If you want to improve in chess, you will have to read books and articles and also analyze your own games. Not every new player can remember all the moves of the game, so this notation system makes it easier.

THE NAMES OF THE SQUARES

When naming a square, we must use the file (letter) and rank (number) to which it belongs. If you've ever played the game Battleship, these coordinates should come easily to you.

SQUARE = FILE + RANK

Can you name all the highlighted squares in the diagram on the right?

It's very important that you write down the file (letter) and then the rank (number) if you want to do it properly. Everyone will still understand what you mean if you say "2d" instead of "d2," but the letters must be lowercase to avoid confusing the pieces with the squares. The abbreviations for the pieces are listed in the chart on the next page.

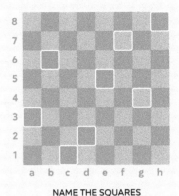

NAME THE SQUARES

ANSWER: a3, b6, c1, d2, e5, f7, g4, h8

WRITE DOWN YOUR MOVE

Bc4

Every piece in chess has its own letter, so we don't have to write down the full name every time.

Piece	Title
King	K
Queen	Q
Rook	R
Bishop	B
Knight	N
Pawn	(nothing)

MOVE = LETTER OF PIECE + SQUARE

The Bishop is moving to c4. In chess notation, this is **Bc4**.

WRITING DOWN A CAPTURE

Writing down a capture is very similar to recording a move, except that we add an *x* in the middle.

CAPTURE = LETTER OF PIECE + *x* + SQUARE

The Queen is capturing the Pawn on f7, checkmate. In chess notation, this is **Qxf7#**.

Why is it checkmate? Remember the ABCs!

A: The Black King can't run **AWAY** to e7 or d7.

B: There is no way to **BLOCK** the check, since the Queen is extremely close.

C: The Queen can't be **CAPTURED** by the King because it is protected by the Bishop on c4.

When a Pawn makes a capture, it's written differently, since we don't include the letter *P* for Pawn. Instead, we put down the file of the Pawn's location, for example, fxe5 = Pawn on the *f* file captures a piece on e5.

WRITE DOWN YOUR CAPTURE

Q x f 7 #

Here are some other important symbols you will need to know:

Symbol	Meaning
x	Capture
+	Check
++	Double check
#	Checkmate
e.p.	En passant
0-0	Kingside castle
0-0-0	Queenside castle
!	Good move
?	Bad move
!!	Excellent move
??	Terrible move
!?	Interesting move
?!	Dubious move
..	Starting with Black's move

READING CHESS NOTATION

In many books, including this one, you will be going through different diagrams. Some will display moves from the very beginning of the game. Some will start in the middle or end of the game.

1. e4 e5

1. = the first move in the diagram

e4 = White's first move

e5 = Black's first move

Since White moves first, their move is always nearest to the move number (i.e., on the left), and Black's move follows (on the right). There will be some cases when diagrams start with Black's move, and the reader won't know White's previous move, so we must write "1. . ."; the ". ." stands for White's previous unknown move.

There are many diagrams in this book, and the text in bold represents how the game or position actually takes place, while text not in bold provides explanations of those moves or alternative moves White or Black might choose to make.

For example:

1. e4 e5 Both Pawns control the center [*explanation of White's and Black's first move*].

2. Bc4 Nc6 Bishop moves to control the center and also to look at the f7 Pawn [*explanation of White's move*]. Another option to play is 2. Qh5 [*states that White had*

SCHOLAR'S MATE

an alternate move]. Black develops their Knight toward the center and to protect the e5 Pawn [*explanation of Black's move*].

3. Qh5 Nf6?? The Queen moves out, and now White has two attackers on the f7 Pawn [*explanation of White's move*]. The King is the only defender. Black should have played **3...Qe7**, which would have saved the game, but didn't realize the threat [*the alternative move Black should have chosen*].

4. Qxf7# Checkmate! This is known as Scholar's Mate (see page 78).

Competitions—Write Down Your Moves

Kids' tournaments (excluding provincial/national events) usually do not require you to write down moves, whereas adult tournaments do. In the next chapter, we will be going over the different types of draws—some of which can be proven only if the moves have been recorded. Writing down the moves is beneficial for you, because in your spare time you can go over the game for a closer look at what you did right or wrong.

I encourage my students to write down their moves any time they participate in an event, because to help them improve, I need to be able to see their strengths and weaknesses. Viewing the records of their games on a regular basis shows me the areas in which they've been improving and those they struggle with. However, if you're just not a fan of writing everything down— even though I recommend it for your own improvement—you can always find a casual chess club in your community. I'm 100 percent sure you will find one.

CHECK, CHECKMATE & DRAWS

Check and Checkmate

The goal of the game is to maneuver your opponent's King into a position where it is under attack, can't move, or can't be helped by its own men. This is also known as checkmate. Check is when the King is under attack but can escape.

The important question: When the King is under attack, what can you or your opponent do? The best way to remember is by using the ABCs.

THE ABCs OF CHECK

AWAY: Run away with the King to a square where it can't be captured.

BLOCK: Put a piece in between the attacker and the King.

CAPTURE: Capture the piece that is attacking the King.

AWAY

DIAGRAM 5.1: The Black King is being checked by the White Rook. The Black King can't move to f8 or h8 because of the Rook, but it can escape to h7 because no White pieces are protecting that square. Black should be losing this position because they have three Pawns (3 points) versus the White Rook (5 points).

DIAGRAM 5.1

DIAGRAM 5.2: The White King is being checked by the Black Bishop. The King can't move to b6, c6, d5, or d6 because of the Queen and/or Bishop. The King can't move to b4, c4, or d4, either, because of the Rook. The King can escape to b5, because no Black pieces are protecting the square. But it's still a losing scenario for White! (White is down 17 points: Q + R + B.)

DIAGRAM 5.2

BLOCK

DIAGRAM 5.3: The White King is being checked by the Queen. The King can't go to a1 or b2 because of the Bishop on f6. The King can't move to a2 because of the Bishop on e6. The King can't go to c2 because of the Queen. There is no White piece capable of capturing the Queen, which is checking the King. The Rook can block the check!

DIAGRAM 5.4: The Black King is being checked by the Rook and therefore cannot move to f8 or h8. The King also can't move to f7 or h7 because of the Pawn. No Black piece can capture the Rook on c8, but luckily, the Black Rook can block the check!

DIAGRAM 5.3

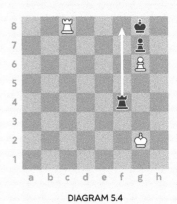

DIAGRAM 5.4

DIAGRAM 5.5

DIAGRAM 5.6

CAPTURE

DIAGRAM 5.5: The Black King is being checked by the Rook. The King can't go to f8 or h8 because of the Rook. It can't go to h7, either, because of the Bishop. Black can't block the check, either—but luckily, the Bishop is able to capture the Rook! White should have thought before making the move Rc8+.

DIAGRAM 5.6: The Black King is being checked by the Queen. The King can't go to g7 or g8 because of the Queen. It can't block the check because it doesn't have any other pieces, but also because the Queen is too close. Luckily, the Queen is unprotected, so the King can simply capture the Queen!

Diagrams 5.1 to 5.6 represent situations in which one side has only one option to save the King. On many occasions, when your King is in check, you might have one, two, or even three options to get out of it. Here are the options I turn to in these circumstances, in order of my preference:

1. **CAPTURE:** Sometimes players get overexcited about a check and don't notice the whole board. Look at the entire board, and see if any pieces can capture the checking piece.

2. **AWAY:** Move that King to a safe square!

3. **BLOCK:** This step should be last, because often when you block the check, your piece's role changes from active to inactive. However, there are always exceptions.

Draws

"Nobody ever won a chess game by resigning."
—Savielly Tartakower

Chess is not always about winning or losing; the game can also be a tie, or draw. Why is it important to know all the types of draws? If you are the winning side (whoever has captured more points), you don't want to tie the game, so you want to be careful not to fall for one of the draws. If you are the losing side, and you really don't see any compensation for the loss of points, it's best to try to trick your opponent into a draw. There are also times when a draw is a mutual decision, not a question of surviving the game at all.

WHAT IS A DRAW?

In a draw, no one wins and no one loses. If you win a round, you get 1 point; if you lose, you get 0 points. You are given 0.5 points for a draw.

There are six types of draws: stalemate, insufficient material, agreement, 50-move rule, perpetual check, and three-time repetition.

Stalemate

Stalemate is when the King is not in check (under attack), but no legal moves or captures can be played. In chess, you are not allowed to skip a turn. If a side does not have any options for legal moves, and the King is not in check, the game cannot continue. Why not? Because the King is not permitted to move into check.

DIAGRAM 5.7

DIAGRAM 5.8

DIAGRAM 5.9

DIAGRAM 5.7: It's White's turn to move, but the King has no options for legal moves. The King is not in check, but White has no other pieces to make a move. It's therefore a stalemate—a draw. White isn't allowed to skip a move, and it's not checkmate.

DIAGRAM 5.8: It's White's turn to move, but the King has no options for legal moves. Again, the King is not in check, but unlike in Diagram 5.7, it's not stalemate, because White still has a legal move: the Pawn.

SACRIFICING TO FORCE STALEMATE

This concept is a little more complex, so I will illustrate it in two diagrams.

DIAGRAM 5.9: It's White's turn to move. The King is not in check and has nowhere to move. The Black Queen is protecting all squares: a1, b2, c2, and c1. The White Pawn can't move or capture. Why is it not stalemate? The White Queen has many possible moves to make. If only we could get rid of the Queen, it would be stalemate. **1. Qg8+!** The Black King must capture the Queen—it is the only move. **1...Kxg8** = stalemate.

DIAGRAM 5.10: It's Black's turn to move. The King is not in check but can still move to g5. The White Queen is protecting g6, g7, h5, and h7. Why is it not stalemate? The King can still move, and the Queen has many possible moves to make. If only we could get rid of the Queen, it would be stalemate, because when White captures the Black Queen, it also protects the g5 square. **1...Qh4+!** The White King must capture the Queen—it is the only move.

Many of my students play **1...Qg4+**, expecting it to force stalemate, but the move makes this only a 50 percent chance. White has two options: to capture the Queen with either the King or the Pawn. If White captures with the King, it forces stalemate. If White captures with the Pawn, it is not stalemate, because the Black King can still move to g5.

DIAGRAM 5.10

Insufficient Material

Situations arise in chess when there are simply not enough pieces to checkmate.

I will be using the letters of the pieces to state positions in which there is insufficient material.

100 PERCENT DRAW

- K versus K
- K versus K + B
- K versus K + N
- K + B versus K + B (Bishops must be on same-colored squares)

DRAWS IF PLAYED CORRECTLY

In the endgame, it's important to leave the King in the center because that's where the King has the most mobility. When the King is in the center, it can access eight squares. If it is on the side of the board, it can reach five squares, and in the corner this number goes down to three. If both sides leave their King in the center, there is no way to checkmate.

- K + N versus K + N
- K + B versus K + N
- K + B versus K + B (Bishops must be on opposite-colored squares)
- K versus K + N + N

Q: WHY IS K VERSUS K + B NOT ENOUGH TO CHECKMATE?

DIAGRAM 5.11: Black's King is under attack, and it can't move to b7 or b8 because of White's King. It can still escape with Ka7. White needs another piece to protect a7 but doesn't have one.

DIAGRAM 5.12: Black's King is trapped: White's Bishop and King prevent it from moving to a2, b1, or b2. It can't be checkmate, though, because the King is not under attack, and no other moves are possible, so this position is stalemate. For this to be checkmate, White needs another Bishop on d4, but they don't have any other piece.

DIAGRAM 5.11

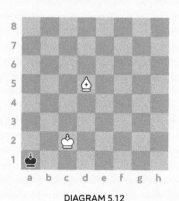

DIAGRAM 5.12

Q: WHY ISN'T K + N VERSUS K + B A 100 PERCENT DRAW?

A side can lose if they bring their King into one of the corners (limiting the King's mobility). There is no way to force a King into the corner (you need more pieces for that), but your opponent might put their own King there (though I doubt it). If a side wanted to lose, they'd have to put their King in the corner, then use their Bishop to eliminate one of their King's options for escape. Diagram 5.13 shows that it is *possible* for a side to lose with these pieces, but if you keep your King in the center, this would never happen!

DIAGRAM 5.13: The White King is checkmated because of the Knight check. It can't move to g2 or h2 because of the Black King.

DIAGRAM 5.13

Agreement

You may offer your opponent a draw. If you'd like to offer a draw the correct way, you must offer it *after* you've made a move.

If you offer it incorrectly (i.e., if it's your turn but you haven't made a move), your opponent can ask you to make a move first and then think about the draw offer. I've had to say this to a few opponents. I don't take the draw right away because my opponent's next move *might* be a mistake and change the outcome of the game. I personally don't penalize people for offering me a draw in an incorrect way—I just let them know the proper format at the end of the game.

When someone offers you a draw, I suggest you say, "Let me think about it," before making your decision. Why? Usually, when someone offers you a draw, it's because (1) they might in fact be in a draw position, or (2) they are weary of their position and hope you'll accept. Chess is a thinking game, so make sure you examine all your options before you agree.

If you agree to a draw, the game has come to an end, and both players get 0.5 points.

If you decline, the game continues.

Tournament facts:

- You can offer a draw a maximum of three times, but I wouldn't be surprised if in some chess events it's as few as one.
- In serious tournaments that offer prize money, you can offer a draw only after 30 or 40 moves (this prevents pre-arranged draws).

50-Move Rule

The 50-move rule goes into effect when no Pawns have been moved or no pieces have been captured in 50 moves. Please note, the only way for you to prove this is by writing down your moves or having an arbiter watch the game.

Why was this rule created? This regulation was put in place for those unable to checkmate without a lot of help from extra pieces. There have been many cases when one side has only a King, while the opponent has a King, Queen, two Rooks, and other pieces yet still doesn't know how to checkmate. We must count 50 moves to ensure the game doesn't go on forever. This also puts the winning side under pressure to create a win in as few moves as possible. If you want to reset the counter, all you need to do is move a Pawn or capture a piece.

WHAT'S WHITE'S BEST MOVE?

DIAGRAM 5.14: It's White's move. White is winning by 5 points. The next move will hit 50 moves in which no captures and no Pawn moves have been made. How do we continue? Move a Pawn (or capture a piece), and the counter restarts!

DIAGRAM 5.14

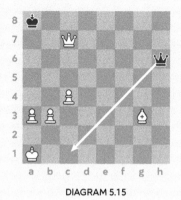

DIAGRAM 5.15

Perpetual Check

This is when the King is repeatedly in check and can't get out of it. When I teach chess to my younger students, I like to call it *infinity* check. Since the game can't go on forever, you can claim a draw once you've produced the position three times. Of course, you must have your moves written down to prove this!

DIAGRAM 5.15: Black to move. White is winning because they are up 6 points and threatening checkmate with Qb8. Black has no hope, except to go with a draw here.

    1. . .Qc1+

    2. Ka2 Qc2+

    3. Ka1 Qc1+

    4. Ka2 Qc2+

    5. Ka1 Qc1+ The position is copied three times.

DIAGRAM 5.16: White to move. Black is winning because they are up 8 points and threatening checkmate: Qf1, Qg1, and Qh2, three different ways! White has no choice—they must go for a draw.

1. **Ng6+ Kh7**

2. **Nf8+ Kh8**

3. **Ng6+ Kh7**

4. **Nf8+ Kh8**

5. **Ng6+ Kh7** The position is copied three times.

DIAGRAM 5.16

Three-Time Repetition

This draw, in Diagram 5.16, is extremely like the one in Diagram 5.15, except no check is involved. The idea is simply that pieces move back and forth while copying the same position three times.

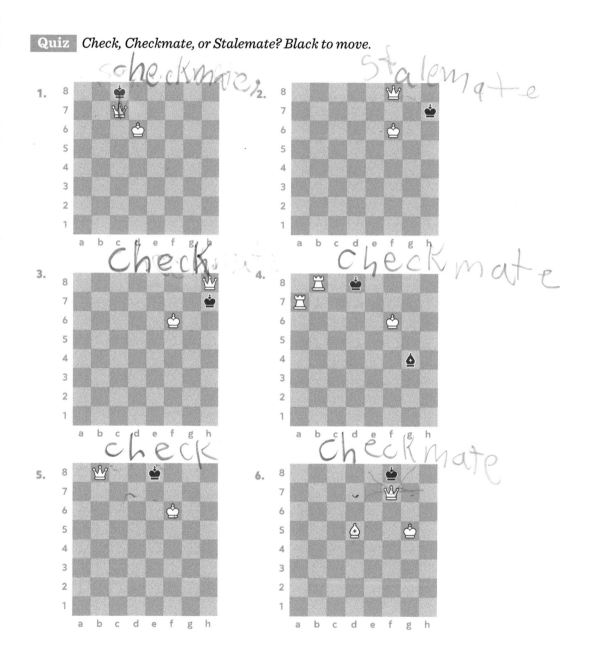

1. *checkmate*

2. *stalemate*

3. *check*

4. *checkmate*

5. *check*

6. *checkmate*

7. *checkmate*

8. *stalemate*

9. *checkmate*

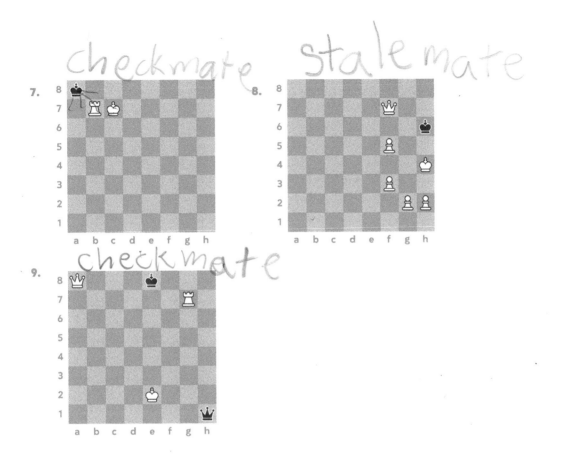

Answers can be found on page 124.

2. Choose Your Strategy

10 ESSENTIAL STRATEGIES & WHY YOU NEED THEM

ABCs of Starting a Game

When starting a chess game, I look out for three things. Yes, another ABC list to remember! Since I have been a chess instructor these past seven years, I continue to find new and better methods, such as these, that help my students remember concepts more effectively.

ACTIVATE your pieces

BRING your King into safety

CONTROL the center

ACTIVATE YOUR PIECES: Bring your Knights and Bishops out! Don't move only Pawns.

BRING YOUR KING INTO SAFETY: Castle your King. Get your King away from the center, where the enemy pieces are waiting to attack.

CONTROL THE CENTER: Control one of the center squares or get your pieces close by.

"Chess is an infinitely complex game, which one can play in infinitely numerous and varied ways."
—Vladimir Kramnik

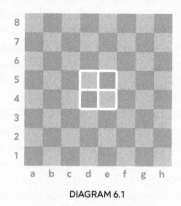

DIAGRAM 6.1

DIAGRAM 6.2

1. Control the Board (Especially the Center)

DIAGRAM 6.1: The more pieces you have in the center, the more control you have of the board. When a piece gets developed in the center, it has more mobility, whereas a piece on the side of the board usually has limited movement.

DIAGRAM 6.2: This is the perfect position White (or Black) would like to achieve. This diagram, however, is not realistic, since it doesn't seem like Black has made any moves yet. I am showing the dream position for every chess player—offering control of the center with all one's pieces. White's next move would be to castle and then move the Queen to e2 or d2 to link the Rooks.

What is a chess opening? A chess opening is a series of moves in the beginning of the game. The opening usually lasts for 10 to 15 moves, and then the middle game starts. There are dozens of different openings and more than 100 variants of each one. Variants are the different moves that can be played after the starting moves. For example, **1. e4 c5** is called the Sicilian Defence opening. All moves following this are called chess variants. 1. e4 c5; 2. Nf3 g6 is now called Sicilian Defence: Hyperaccelerated Dragon variant. For each variant, there's a code.

I wouldn't worry too much about openings until you are fairly familiar with the rules of the game. The following diagrams, 6.3 and 6.4, illustrate two common openings.

FOUR KNIGHTS GAME: ITALIAN VARIATION C50

DIAGRAM 6.3:

DIAGRAM 6.3

1. e4 e5 White Pawn to e4, Black Pawn to e5. Both Pawns protect the center.

2. Nf3 Nc6 White Knight to f3, Black Knight to c6. Develop the Knights toward the center, where they control more squares, unlike their positions at the sides of the board.

3. Bc4 Bc5 White Bishop to c4, Black Bishop to c5. Develop the Bishops to protect the center and surrounding squares. The Bishops eye each other's weaknesses, the f Pawns, but also open the way for their Kings to castle.

4. 0-0 Nf6 Kingside castle, Black Knight to f6. Castle the King. Black will castle on the following move, because they must develop their Knight first (which also attacks the e4 Pawn).

5. Nc3 0-0 White Knight to c3, kingside castle. White develops their Knight and protects the e4 Pawn. Both sides now control the center and have castled their Kings. Next, they must develop their Bishops, but the Pawns are blocking the way.

6. d3 h6 White Pawn to d3, Black Pawn to h6. Black stops White from developing the Bishop to g5, while creating a fleeing square for their King in the future.

DIAGRAM 6.4

QUEEN'S PAWN GAME: CHIGORIN VARIATION D02

DIAGRAM 6.4:

1. d4 d5 White Pawn to d4, Black Pawn to d5

2. Nf3 Nc6 White Knight to f3, Black Knight to c6

3. Bf4 Nf6 White Bishop to f4, Black Knight to f6

4. Nc3 Bf5 White Knight to c3, Black Bishop to f5

5. e3 e6 White Pawn to e3, Black Pawn to e6

6. Bb5 Bd6 White Bishop to b5, Black Bishop to d6

At this point in the game, most of White's and Black's pieces are out. On the next move, both sides are ready to castle their Kings.

Quiz 1 *Which pieces are not developed correctly?*

Answer can be found on page 125.

2. Don't Give Up Your Pieces Easily

One of the most important concepts for beginners in chess is understanding the values of the different pieces—this allows you to calculate when to capture pieces and when to hold back. After all, you don't want to give your opponent unnecessary gifts—this will only help them beat you!

Piece	Points
King	Game
Queen	9
Rook	5
Bishop	3
Knight	3
Pawn	1

HANGING PIECES

The term *hanging* in chess means unprotected. Therefore, an unprotected piece is known as a hanging piece.

"The beauty of chess is it can be whatever you want it to be. It transcends language, age, race, religion, politics, gender, and socioeconomic background. Whatever your circumstances, anyone can enjoy a good fight to the death over the chess board."
— Simon Williams

DIAGRAM 6.6

DIAGRAM 6.6: Black just moved their Knight to g4, in hopes of capturing the Bishop on e3. The problem is the Black Knight moved onto a square where it's not protected by one of its own. The White Queen can simply capture the Knight for free: Qxg4.

CAPTURING PROTECTED PIECES

When capturing protected pieces, a little bit of mental math is involved.

PIECE YOU CAPTURED – PIECE YOU GAVE UP = EQUAL, LOSING, OR WINNING POINTS.

DIAGRAM 6.7: Both sides possess the same amount of points. It's White's turn to move, and the Knight is attacking four pieces at once, but they are all protected. Which one should the Knight capture?

DIAGRAM 6.7: WHITE TO MOVE

Nxb5 The Queen is worth 9 points. If the Knight captures the Queen, White will lose their Knight because of the Pawn or Rook. Math: 9 – 3 = 6. White wins 6 points and the strongest piece!

Nxc6 The Pawn is worth 1 point. If the Knight captures the Pawn, White will lose their Knight because of the Pawn. Math: 1 – 3 = –2 points. White loses 2 points for capturing a weaker piece.

Nxe6 The Bishop is worth 3 points. If the Knight captures the Rook, White will lose their Knight because of the Pawn. Math: 3 – 3 = 0. This is called a trade (equal). No one wins or loses points.

Nxf5 The Rook is worth 5 points. If the Knight captures the Rook, White will lose their Knight because of the Bishop. Math: 5 – 3 = 2. White wins 2 points for capturing a stronger piece.

Answer: The best capture for the Knight is the Queen on b5, which will win them 6 points.

DIAGRAM 6.8: White is down 1 point. It's White's turn to move, and the Bishop is attacking two pieces at the same time: the protected Rook and hanging Knight.

Bxa8 The Rook is worth 5 points. If the Bishop captures the Rook, White will lose their Bishop because of the other Rook on f8. Math: 5 –3 = 2. White wins 2 points for capturing a stronger (but protected) piece.

Bxb5 The Knight is worth 3 points. If the Bishop captures the Knight, White won't lose any points, since the Knight is not protected by any of Black's pieces. Math: 3 – 0 = 3. White wins 3 points for capturing an unprotected piece.

DIAGRAM 6.8: WHITE TO MOVE

TRADING PIECES

A trade takes place when a piece of the same value captures a protected piece of the same value, for example, Queen for Queen, Knight for Bishop, or Pawn for Pawn.

Reasons for trades:

- When you are ahead in material, to remove any of your opponent's pieces that can potentially counterattack your plans
- When there are open files/ranks/diagonals
- To remove a piece defending certain squares

When you decide to trade a piece, make sure you don't give up a strong one (with more mobility) for a weak one (with less mobility).

EXCEPTIONS

Many games in chess include opportunities for sacrifice. A sacrifice is when you give up material to checkmate or gain more at the end.

DIAGRAM 6.9: Black is down two Pawns but still maintains a strong position. The Queen and Bishop are eyeing the h2 Pawn, which is doubly protected by the King and the Knight.

1. . .Rxf3! Black Rook captures Knight on f3. Black captures the protected Knight on f3! Why on earth would Black give up a 5-point piece for a 3-point piece? The Knight is protecting checkmate on h2. This is also called *removing the guard* or *removing the defender*. White's best move is to play 2. g3 to protect against the threat. But then Black will respond with 2. . .Rd3, getting the Rook to safety (i.e., the Rook will be protected by the Queen) and a winning advantage for capturing White's Knight for free.

DIAGRAM 6.9

2. Qxf3?? Qxh2# White Queen captures Knight on f3 (terrible move). Black Queen captures Pawn on h2, checkmate. White is checkmated. The King can't run away to h1 because it's protected by the Queen. The King can't capture the Queen because it's protected by the Bishop. There is no blocking possible here, since the Queen is too close to the King. This is a good example of how every move requires you to think ahead to its consequences. In this case, capturing the Rook seemed like a very straightforward idea but turned out to have a negative outcome.

"Chess is the gymnasium of the mind."
—Blaise Pascal

Quiz 2 *What's the best capture for White? What's the best capture for Black?*

Answers can be found on page 125.

3. Ask Yourself Why

Whenever I play a game of chess, I always ask myself why my opponent made the move. It doesn't matter if I'm playing against a weaker or stronger player. Weak players can still make occasional strong moves, and strong players can make mistakes. That's what makes us *human*.

When your opponent makes a move, ask yourself these three questions:

1. Is the piece that just moved attacking anything?

2. Are any of the other pieces attacking mine?

3. Did the piece that just moved stop protecting another piece or stop protecting against a threat?

MOVE: ATTACK

If your opponent made a move, and your piece is now under attack, first see if you can capture it with an equal-value or lower-value piece. If no capture is possible, move it away, unless it's the same or higher value as the attacker; in that case, you can also protect it. If the attacker is a lower-value piece, you most likely want to move your piece.

DIAGRAM 6.12:

Why did Black make this move? Are they attacking anything?

Black is attacking the Knight. White can't simply protect their Knight because the attacker is a lower-ranked piece. If 1. Be3 exd4, then White losing a Knight for a Pawn would equal −2 points. We must do something about the Knight.

DIAGRAM 6.13:

What should White do now?

The Knight can move to b3, b5, e2, f3, or f5, or capture the Knight on c6 (a trade). It can't leave the Knight on the square or move it to e6 because of the d7 and f7 Pawns.

Why did Black make this move?

Black is attacking the Knight. White has multiple possibilities—Ne4, Nf3, and Rd1 to get the Knight out of danger—but sees that when the Queen made the move, it stopped protecting the Rook. Who cares about our 3-point piece if we can capture a 5-point one? **1. Qxc7**.

Quiz 3 *Why did White make this move? What should be Black's next move?*

DIAGRAM 6.12

DIAGRAM 6.13

Answers can be found on page 125.

DIAGRAM 6.15

DIAGRAM 6.16

MOVE: NO ATTACK

If your opponent made a move and none of your pieces are under attack by that piece, see if it was protecting another piece or protecting against a threat. A lot of beginner chess players forget about pieces they were defending earlier. (See **DIAGRAM 6.15**.)

White moved the Knight. Is it attacking anything? No. The Pawn on c6 is protected by the Pawn and Queen. Was the Knight defending anything? Yes. It used to protect the other Knight.

1. Nd4?? Bxd2 Black moved the Knight. Is it attacking anything? No. Was it protecting anything? Yes. It used to protect the e8 square, so now White is able to checkmate: **1. . .Nd5**; **2. Re8#**. (See **DIAGRAM 6.16**.)

Quiz 4 *What's the best move for Black?*

Answer can be found on page 125.

4. Look at the Whole Board

In my opinion, this strategy is critical, and many beginner players fail to consider it. If you scan the whole board before and after your move, you will make fewer mistakes. I have failed to remember this advice myself on certain occasions. During those games, I was so focused on one side of the board, I didn't notice my opponent's attack on the other.

Scanning the board before and after your move gives you a much better chance of noticing:

- unexpected attacks on your pieces
- potential attacks you can make on your opponent's pieces
- pieces and threats that are no longer protected by your opponent

Yelizaveta Orlova – N.N.

1. b3 g6 White Pawn to b3, Black Pawn to g6

2. Bb2 Nf6? White Bishop to b2, Black Knight to f6 (bad move)

3. f4 d5 White Pawn to f4, Black Pawn to d5

4. Nf3 c5 White Knight to f3, Black Pawn to c5

5. e3 Ne4?? White Pawn to e3, Black Knight to e4 (terrible move) (See **DIAGRAM 6.18**.)

Black's move, at a glance, seems good. The Knight is located on a center square; it's guarded by the Pawn on d5, and none of White's pieces can capture it.

DIAGRAM 6.18

When Black looks at the whole board, however, they notice that the Bishop on b2 is attacking the Rook on h8, which also happens to be unprotected!

Bxh8! White Bishop captures Rook on h8 (bad move). If White had only focused on the piece that just moved (and not the entire board), they wouldn't have won 5 points!

Quiz 5 *What's the best move for Black?*

Answer can be found on page 125.

5. Protect Your King

As discussed in the castling section earlier, the King is vulnerable in the center of the board, unless it's in the endgame. You wouldn't want your King hanging around your opponent's pieces. Castling either kingside or queenside will get your King away from the center. There are rare exceptions when top players don't castle, but in 99 percent of games, castling is involved.

CASTLE AS QUICKLY AS POSSIBLE

The longer you keep your King in the center, the more likely it will be in danger. Try to castle in the first 10 moves of the game.

Here is a nice example, called Legal's Mate, which involves keeping the Black King in the center (while the White King is one move away):

1. e4 e5 White Pawn to e4, Black Pawn to e5. Both Pawns control the center.

2. Nf3 d6 White Knight to f3, Black Pawn to d6. The White Knight attacks the Pawn on e5, and Black defends differently than usual. More common is the move **2. . .Nc6**.

DIAGRAM 6.20

3. Bc4 Bg4 White Bishop to c4, Black Bishop to g4. White and Black develop their Bishops. White's Bishop eyes the f7 Pawn, but it's protected by the King. Black's Bishop pins White's Knight, which can't move because the Queen is behind. The Queen and Pawn are protecting the Knight, which means if the Bishop captures the Knight, the next move will result in a trade. Black captures a 3-point piece, and White captures a 3-point piece, as well.

4. Nc3 g6? White Knight to c3, Black Pawn to g6 (bad move). Black doesn't see the next move coming . . . but before we get there, let's analyze this position. White has developed three strong pieces, the two Knights and the Bishop, while Black has developed only the Bishop. Which side is about to castle? White, because the Bishop and Knight are no longer in the way. (See **DIAGRAM 6.20**.)

5. Nxe5!! Bxd1?? White Knight captures Pawn on e5 (excellent move), Black Bishop captures Queen on d1 (terrible move). Why would the Knight capture the protected Pawn? Not only that, but allow Black to capture their Queen? If Black captures the Knight, 5. . .dxe5; 6. Qxg4. White captures both a Pawn and a Bishop, while Black has captured only a Knight. Therefore, White wins a Pawn—this move is better than Black's, but White is too greedy and goes for the Queen!

6. Bxf7+ Ke7 White Bishop captures Pawn on f7, check, Black King to e7. The King can't capture the Bishop or move to d7.

7. Nd5# White Knight to d5, checkmate. Checkmate! A really beautiful example of keeping the King in the center. Yes, White's King is also not castled yet, but they can do so on any next move. (See **DIAGRAM 6.21**.)

DIAGRAM 6.21

CREATE A FLEEING SQUARE

When you castle kingside, you should move your h Pawn to give more space to the King. Many players don't create a fleeing point and end up falling for the back-rank checkmate (see Check and Checkmate, page 40). (See **DIAGRAM 6.22**.)

Black's last move was Pawn to h6. This move is to prevent the Bishop from moving to g5 but also to let the King breathe and provide the possibility to escape to h7, if needed.

DIAGRAM 6.22

FIANCHETTO BISHOP

A fianchetto bishop is the development of your Bishop on the longest diagonal (either a1 to h8 or a8 to h1), while hiding it in a fortress of Pawns. I really like to call the fianchetto bishop "the sniper," since it hides and waits for the right moment to strike! At the very beginning of the game, the Bishop doesn't seem particularly strong, but once other pieces are traded off and diagonals open up, it becomes a monster. (See **DIAGRAM 6.23**.)

So why is the fianchetto bishop in this section of the book?

The fianchetto bishop can serve as extra protection for the King, but it can also stop back-rank checkmate. It can stop this by acting as a blockader; once the Bishop has moved, the King will have a fleeing square.

DIAGRAM 6.23

Take care not to trade off your fianchetto bishop for your opponent's Knight, or you will leave a hole in your King's castle.

I always encourage my students to play with fianchetto bishops from time to time. Young boys are particularly encouraged to try them when they hear I call these snipers, as a lot of them play video games.

Quiz 6 *How can White escape from check in each scenario?*

Answers can be found on page 126.

6. Use All Your Pieces

Make sure all your pieces are out and ready to fight! If your Knight hasn't moved yet, and it's been 10 moves, move it next! Imagine you're playing on a soccer team, but two teammates are just sitting on the field doing nothing. Will the team do well against the opposing team who has all team members participating in the game? Of course not. Similar to soccer, chess requires teamwork! The majority of checkmates don't succeed using just one piece—on the contrary, it takes multiple pieces assisting in the attack.

Emanuel Lasker was a German Grandmaster and 27-time World Champion. Lasker is the only person to hold the World Champion title that long. The following game bearing his name is extremely renowned—today, it's still considered one of the best checkmates! (See **DIAGRAM 6.26**.)

DIAGRAM 6.26

1. Qxh7 Kxh7 White Queen captures Pawn on h7, Black King captures Queen on h7. Oh, Lord! White sacrifices their Queen for a Pawn. Why? We shall see . . .

2. Nxf6++ Kh6 White Knight captures Bishop on f6, double check, Black King to h6. It's double check. The King's only response is to move. The Knight can't be captured because the Bishop is still attacking the King. If 2. . . Kh8, 3. Ng6# (2. . .Black King to h8; 3. White Knight to g6, checkmate).

3. Ng4+ Kg5 White Knight to g4, check, King to g5. Bringing in another Knight (second piece) to the attack!

4. h4+ Kf4 White Pawn to h4, check, Black King to f4. Third piece . . .

5. g3+ Kf3 White Pawn to g3, check, Black King to f3 Fourth piece . . .

6. Be2+ Kg2 White Bishop to e2, check, Black King to g2. Luring Black more into White's camp.

7. Rh2+ Kg1 White Rook to h2, check, Black King to g1. Now the Rooks come in.

8. Kd2# White King to d2, checkmate. Beautiful checkmate. White used their pieces as a team to achieve the goal. (See **DIAGRAM 6.27**.)

DIAGRAM 6.27

7. Think Several Moves Ahead

Thinking several moves ahead is extremely important in chess, and it mostly comes with practice. I did many chess puzzles as a kid: both checkmate problems (in x amount of moves) and tactical ones. In my spare time, I read many books on tactics, strategy, and endgame concepts. However, you can't become a stronger player by studying alone—playing chess against others allows you to implement what you have learned.

1. c4 e5 White Pawn to c4, Black Pawn to c4. Both starting moves are great. White protects the d5 center square, and Black protects the d4 center square.

2. e3 Bb4 White Pawn to e3, Black Bishop to b4. White's move opens up the way for the Bishop. Black develops their Bishop but not on the best square, since it's not really accomplishing anything there. (See **DIAGRAM 6.28**.)

3. a3 Ba5?? White Pawn to a3, Bishop to a5 (terrible move). White attacks the Bishop and gains a tempo, or gains time. Black loses a tempo because it just developed the Bishop and has to move it again instead of another piece. Black's move is a big mistake because they're moving onto a square where the Bishop will have limited mobility; after Ba5, the piece has only one square to which it can move. Now, White can trap the Bishop in two moves. 3...Bishop to e7 would have been a much better move.

4. b4! Bb6 White Pawn to b4 (good move), Black Bishop to b6.

5. c5! White Pawn to c5 (good move). (See **DIAGRAM 6.29**.) White will win the Bishop for a Pawn. Yay!

DIAGRAM 6.28

DIAGRAM 6.29

8. Go for a Quick Checkmate

WEAKEST PAWN

The weakest Pawns in the starting position are the f2 Pawn for White and the f7 Pawn for Black. These are vulnerable because they are the only Pawns (out of eight) protected *only* by the King. If these Pawns have one attacker and one defender, they're not safe enough to capture. On the other hand, if White or Black manages to add a second attacker, so they have two pieces attacking these Pawns (still with only one defender), they will be easy enough to capture.

SCHOLAR'S MATE

Scholar's Mate is the four-move checkmate strategy. (In Russian, it's called Kid's Mate.) If you play against a beginner, I'd suggest trying it out once, but I doubt you will be able to use it a second time against the same opponent!

1. e4 e5 White Pawn to e4, Black Pawn to e5. Good starting moves by both sides.

2. Qh5 Nc6 White Queen to h5, Black Knight to c6. White's Queen is attacking the e5 Pawn (without defenders) and putting pressure on the f7 Pawn (can't capture the Pawn, protected by the King). The Black Knight moves to c6 to defend the e5 Pawn. It would be terrible to lose the Queen for capturing a protected Pawn, as the Queen is worth 9 points, and the Pawn is only worth 1.

3. Bc4 Nf6?? White Bishop to c4, Black Knight to f6 (terrible move). White develops their Bishop to c4 to attack the f7 Pawn. The f7 Pawn is now under attack twice (by the Queen and Bishop), and there is only one defender (the King). Black must protect the Pawn a second time but fails to see the threat—instead, they play Nf6 to attack the Queen.

4. Qxf7# White Queen captures Pawn on f7, checkmate. (See **DIAGRAM 6.30**.) Checkmate! The Queen is checking the King and protecting square e7. The King can't capture the Queen because it's protected by the Bishop.

Another way to get to the same position:

1. e4 e5 White Pawn to e4, Black Pawn to e5.

2. Bc4 Nc6 White Bishop to c4, Black Knight to c6.

3. Qh5 Nf6?? White Queen to h5, Black Knight to f6 (terrible move).

4. Qxf7# White Queen to f7, checkmate.

DIAGRAM 6.30

DIAGRAM 6.31

Common mistake

1. e4 e5 White Pawn to e4, Black Pawn to e5.

2. Qh5 g6?? White Queen to h5, Black Pawn to g6 (terrible move). (See **DIAGRAM 6.31**.) Black makes a mistake by not protecting the e5 Pawn and opening the a1-to-h8 diagonal.

3. Qxe5! Be7 White Queen captures Pawn on e5 (good move), Bishop to e7. White captures the Pawn and attacks the King and Rook at the same time. Black must protect the King by blocking, since the King can't run away without being captured.

4. Qxh8 White Queen captures Rook on h8. White is up 6 points and should win the game.

HOW TO PROTECT AGAINST SCHOLAR'S MATE

It depends on how White starts the Scholar's Mate: (1) if they bring out the Queen first and then the Bishop, or (2) if they bring out the Bishop first and then the Queen.

Queen, then Bishop

1. e4 e5 White Pawn to e4, Black Pawn to e5.

2. Qh5 Nc6 White Queen to h5, Black Knight to c6. White Queen eyes the f7 Pawn and attacks the e5 Pawn. Black develops their Knight and protects the Pawn.

3. Bc4 Qe7! White Bishop to c4, Black Queen to e7 (good move). (See **DIAGRAM 6.32**.) Bishop develops to c4 and attacks the f7 Pawn, so now there are two attackers

DIAGRAM 6.32

(Bishop and Queen) and one defender (King). Black adds a defender to f7 by moving their Queen. It's not a good idea for White to capture the f7 Pawn, because they would lose material: **4. Bxf7?? Qxf7; 5. Qxf7 Kxf7** (4. White Bishop captures Black Pawn on f7 [bad move], Black Queen captures White Bishop on f7; 5. White Queen captures Black Queen on f7, Black King captures White Queen on f7), and Black is now ahead by 2 points.

4. Nc3 Nf6 White Knight to c3, Black Knight to f6. Black has now successfully stopped White's plan and drives off the Queen while developing their Knight.

Bishop, then Queen

This one is simple: Black shouldn't allow the White Queen to move to h5!

1. e4 e5 White Pawn to e4, Black Pawn to e5.

2. Bc4 Nf6 White Bishop to c4, Black Knight to f6. (See **DIAGRAM 6.33**.)

DIAGRAM 6.33

That's all you have to do! There's no reason for White to play the move Qf3 (and not attack any piece at all) or the horrible move Qh5 (which loses the Queen).

FOOL'S MATE

The shortest checkmate is called Fool's Mate, but this one you can't force. Even a beginner would have to be very unlucky to make the worst two moves, when there are so many options to choose from in the starting position. Try not to move your f Pawn, whether you are playing White or

Black, when you're a beginner at chess, or you might accidentally fall for this!

1. f3? e5 White Pawn to f3 (bad move), black Pawn to e5. White's first move doesn't seem so bad, since it's protecting the e4 center square, but it's preventing the Knight from developing to f3, and it opens the e1-to-h4 diagonal. Black moves to e5 to protect the center and open the diagonal for the Queen.

2. g4?? Qh4# White Pawn to g4 (terrible move), Black Queen to h4, checkmate. (See **DIAGRAM 6.34**.) White makes an enormous blunder! The Pawn on g2 was the only piece to protect against the Queen's check. Black checkmates with 2...Qh4#: There is no way to run away with the King, block, or capture the checking piece.

DIAGRAM 6.34

Quiz 7 *What's another way the White queen can attack the f7 pawn?*

Answer can be found on page 126.

9. Try a Fried Liver Attack

The Fried Liver Attack is a sequence of moves White can use to potentially win material at the beginning of the game. Black has only *one* correct response to this—the reason many players take the chance of playing it.

1. e4 e5 White Pawn to e4, Black Pawn to e5. Both Pawns control the center.

2. Nf3 Nc6 White Knight to f3, Black Knight to c6. White attacks the e5 Pawn. Black defends with the Knight.

3. Bc4 Nf6 White Bishop to c4, Black Knight to f6. Bishop develops position to eye the f7 Pawn. Black develops the Knight and attacks the e4 Pawn.

4. Ng5! White Knight to g5 (good move). (See **DIAGRAM 6.36**.) White protects the e5 Pawn and attacks the f7 Pawn simultaneously. White now has two attackers on f7, while Black has one defender. Black's best and *only* response to defend f7 is: **4...d5!** Black Pawn to d5 (good move). (See **DIAGRAM 6.37**.)

DIAGRAM 6.36

DIAGRAM 6.37

Black blocks the Bishop's diagonal, and now there's only one attacker and one defender on the f7 Pawn. The d5 Pawn has two attackers but also two defenders, which means if White decides to capture it, this will end up being a trade. For example, 5. exd5 Nxd5; 6. Bxd5 Qxd5 (White Pawn captures Pawn on d5, Black Knight captures Pawn on d5; 6. White Bishop captures Knight on d5, Queen captures Bishop on d5).

If Black ignores the Fried Liver Attack

1. e4 e5 White Pawn to e4, Black Pawn to e5.

2. Nf3 Nc6 White Knight to f3, Black Knight to c6.

3. Bc4 Nf6 White Bishop to c4, Black Knight to f6.

4. Ng5! h6? White Knight to g5 (good move), Black Pawn to h6 (bad move).

DIAGRAM 6.38

5. Nxf7! White Knight captures Pawn on g7 (good move). (See **DIAGRAM 6.38**.) The Black King can't capture the White Knight because it's protected by the Bishop; at the same time, the Knight is making a double attack (fork) on the Queen and Rook. Since the Queen is valued higher than the Rook, Black will therefore need to move their Queen and lose the Rook.

6. ..Qe7 Black Queen to e7.

White Knight captures Rook on h8 (Nxh8). White should win this game, being up 6 points from the very beginning!

Quiz 8 *Is it safe for White to play Nxf7?*

Answer can be found on page 126.

10. Find an Advantage

There are five points I consistently refer to whenever I don't have a tactical move to win material or checkmate. These help me devise a plan whenever one doesn't immediately come to mind.

1. **MATERIAL ADVANTAGE**

2. **KING SAFETY**

3. **PAWN STRUCTURE**

4. **SPACE/TERRITORY**

5. **PIECE MOBILITY**

MATERIAL ADVANTAGE

This is the most obvious advantage, and disadvantage, in chess. This is what you should think about if you are the winning or losing side.

Winning Side

TRADE PIECES. The more of your opponent's pieces you eliminate, the less you have to worry about.

TRADE QUEENS. Get rid of your opponent's strongest attacker, unless you need your own for a winning attack.

"Play the opening like a book, the middlegame like a magician, and the endgame like a machine."
—Rudolph Spielmann

DIAGRAM 6.40

DON'T BE OVERCONFIDENT. "The game isn't over 'til it's over!" Play your best until the end. If you let your guard down, you might make mistakes and change the outcome of the game.

IF YOU'RE IN A BAD SITUATION, your King is open, and your opponent seems to have a strong attack, you can always give up some material to get your King to safety. (See **DIAGRAM 6.40**.)

White is winning by 3 points, but Black's move is a little scary. Black is making a double attack (fork) on the Queen and threatening Qh2 checkmate. How should White defend against this? Trade Queens! Black's main attacker is the Queen, so since White is ahead in material, White benefits from the trade.

Losing Side

DON'T TRADE. The more pieces you have on the board, the greater your chances to initiate a strong attack.

DON'T ALWAYS LOOK FOR A WAY TO WIN. Make sure to always be thinking about draws, too. It's better to tie the game than lose.

SOMETIMES IT'S GOOD TO SACRIFICE MATERIAL to gain access to your opponent's King. You're already losing, so why not make the game interesting with a strong attack? If you're only a Pawn or two down, I wouldn't suggest going overboard, but if you're down a Rook or more, I'd go full out!

Below is an interesting scenario where Black was completely winning but didn't see White's threat. But first, let's answer this question:

Quiz 9 *Black is clearly winning here, but by how many points?*

Answer can be found on page 126.

1. ..QF4?? Black Queen to f4 (terrible move). A horrible move that sadly loses the game.

2. Qb3+ Kh8 White Queen to b3, Black King to h8. Black can't block the check or they will just lose material. Black can't play 2...Kf8 because of 3. Qf7#.

3. Nf7+ Kg8 White Knight to f7, check, Black King to g8. White brings the Knight into the attack! Black's only response is Kg8.

4. Nh6++ Kh8 White Knight to h6, double check, Black King to h8. Same as before, the King can't move: Black King to f8, White Queen to f7, checkmate (4...Kf8; 5. Qf7#).

"Tactics is knowing what to do when there is something to do; strategy is knowing what to do when there is nothing to do."
—Savielly Tartakower

5. Qg8+!! Rxg8 White Queen to g8, check (excellent move), Rook captures Queen on g8. Absolutely amazing move by White. This leads to a smothered mate. (A smothered mate is when the King is surrounded by his own pieces, which restricts the King's movement.) Notice: 5. . .Kxg8 is not possible because the Queen is protected by the Knight—only the Rook can capture it.

6. Nf7# Black Rook takes Queen on f7, checkmate.

KING SAFETY

Make sure to observe your opponent's King (and yours) at all times! If your King is castled, but your opponent's King isn't, how can you keep theirs in the center and prevent them from castling? Your opponent just moved a Pawn near their King, and now the King is more open, so find ways to destroy the defense and open it even further! Are some of your pieces nearby the King? If so, can you bring in more pieces to start an attack?

Don't forget about your own King! If the King is slightly open, or there are opponent's pieces nearby, this is probably a sign you must go into defense mode!

White is up a Pawn, which is also a passed pawn. A passed pawn is a Pawn that can't be stopped by an opponent's Pawns to get to the promotional rank. The problem for White is that the Black Rook is on a2, which is looking toward the King. We will take a look at this position from both perspectives. (See **DIAGRAM 6.42**.)

DIAGRAM 6.42

Black to move

Black knows they are down a Pawn, so if they don't do anything aggressive, they will lose the game. The Rook on a2 is very strong and eyeing the g2 Pawn, which at the moment is protected until Black adds another attacker. Black notices that most of White's strong pieces are positioned on the queenside, far from the King. If it were Black's turn to move, it wouldn't end well for White!

1. . .Qg5 Black Queen to g5. This adds another attacker on the g2 Pawn and threatens Qxg2#. White can't protect the Pawn with another piece without losing material. (If 2. Qf2 Rxf2, Black will be up 3 points in a Queen-versus-Rook endgame.)

2. g4 Qd2 White Pawn to g4, Black Queen to d2. The only move for White. Black continues with their threat on checkmate with their last move: Qg2#. Black Queen to g2, checkmate.

There are a few possible endings:

#1

3. Kf1 Qe2+ White King to f1, Black Queen to e2, check.

4. Kg1 Qg2# White King to g1, Black Queen to g2, checkmate. (See **DIAGRAM 6.43**.)

DIAGRAM 6.43

DIAGRAM 6.44

DIAGRAM 6.45

#2

3. Qf2 Qxf2+ White Queen to f2, Black Queen captures Queen on f2, check.

4. Kh1 Qg2# White King to h1, Black Queen to g2, checkmate. (See **DIAGRAM 6.44**.)

#3

3. Rb2 Ra1+ White Rook to b2, Black Rook to a1, check.

4. Rb1 Rxb1# White Rook to b1, Black Rook captures Rook, checkmate. (See **DIAGRAM 6.45**.)

White to move

In the actual game, it was White to move. Botvinnik found the best move to stop his opponent's threat: 1. . .Qg5.

1. Qe3! White Queen to e3. The Queen protects the g5 square, to which Black is still welcome to move, but when you're down material, you don't want to trade pieces. White also opens up the way for the c Pawn to eventually promote!

PAWN STRUCTURE

Pawn structure weaknesses are isolated pawns, double/ triple pawns, and pawn islands. There are exceptions when these weaknesses can help in different parts of the game.

Isolated Pawns

Isolated pawns are Pawns that aren't being protected by other Pawns. Isolated pawns are usually an inconvenience, because you have to use your strong pieces as defenders when they could be of better use somewhere else. If you want to get rid of an isolated pawn, look for a way to trade it with a Pawn of your opponent's.

In **DIAGRAM 6.46**, White's Pawn on d4 is isolated. There is no Pawn on the c or e file to protect it.

Black's Pawns on b5 and h5 are isolated for the same reason. Because of this, both sides' Pawn structure isn't the best.

Double/Triple Pawns

Double pawns are two Pawns positioned on the same file. Similarly, triple pawns are three Pawns on the same file. Technically speaking, it is possible to get quadruple pawns in chess, but it is rare. I feel like this is self-explanatory, such as in the following example:

DIAGRAM 6.46

| Quiz 10 | *Which pawns are doubled and tripled?*

Answer can be found on page 126.

Pawn Islands

While isolated pawns are individual unprotected pawns, pawn islands are groups of Pawns connected by files. The more pawn islands among your pieces, the weaker your pawn structure, as they offer more targets for your opponent. A pawn base is the first Pawn in a pawn chain (or string of Pawns) not protected by another Pawn. The more pawn islands you have, the more pawn bases you have, as well.

Two Pawn Islands versus Two Pawn Islands

White has two pawn islands, because there's no Pawn on the e file: (1) a2, b3, c4, d5 and (2) f4, g3, h2. (See **DIAGRAM 6.48**.)

Black has two pawn islands, because there's no Pawn on the e file and f file: (1) a5, b6, c7, d6 and (2) g4, g6, h5.

White's pawn bases are a2 and h2. These Pawns are going to be a target, and White will have to use higher-ranked pieces to protect it. Black's pawn bases are c7 and g6.

One Pawn Island versus Two Pawn Islands

In **DIAGRAM 6.49**, White's pawn structure is more promising because it has fewer weaknesses. White has one pawn island and no isolated or double/triple pawns. Black has two pawn islands, which will later become two weaknesses, plus the double pawns are really not favorable, either. One benefit of the double pawns (in this diagram), however, is that the e file is open for a Rook. That's what I mean about every pawn weakness having exceptions. Trading pawn weakness for greater mobility of another piece is worth it most of the time!

DIAGRAM 6.48

DIAGRAM 6.49

Three Pawn Islands versus Four Pawn Islands

Black's pawn structure is the superior one in **DIAGRAM 6.50** because it has fewer weaknesses. To be honest, I don't like either side here, but Black's position is slightly stronger. White has four pawn islands, and three of the islands are isolated pawns. The pawn base on e3 is definitely a target, too. Black has three pawn islands, two pawn bases, and only one isolated pawn.

DIAGRAM 6.50

Quiz 11 *Why are isolated pawns to be avoided?*

Answer can be found on page 126.

Whose pawn structure is better in DIAGRAM 6.51?

If you answered Black, you are correct! White has four pawn weakness compared to Black, which only has two. White's a4 Pawn is isolated, c2-c3 are doubled, and it has three pawn islands. White's h Pawn is weak because it's the base of the pawn chain. Black has only two weaknesses: the pawn bases on a7 and f7.

NOTE: If you have any of these pawn weaknesses, it doesn't mean you're losing; I am simply trying to point out that you will have more weaknesses for your opponent to target.

DIAGRAM 6.51

DIAGRAM 6.52

DIAGRAM 6.53

SPACE/TERRITORY

When it comes to space on the board, the more you have, the greater your advantage in the game. (See **DIAGRAM 6.52**.)

(MORE) SPACE = (MORE) PIECE MOBILITY = (MORE) PLANS

More space on the chessboard equals more movement for your pieces. If your pieces display a lot more movement compared to those of your opponent, this leads to more ambitious plans you can carry out against them. When a side has little space, they can barely move their pieces, and they usually find they don't have many options for moves.

Space can help you distinguish what strategy you are going to choose.

DIAGRAM 6.53 is a position from one of my games. Playing Black, I have more space on the kingside, so my plan is to form an attack by playing g5-g4. This will weaken my own King but target my opponent's King, as well. White's plan is to play on the queenside since their Pawns are more advanced on that part of the board. In the next section, you will see their position at the end of this game.

PIECE MOBILITY

As stated above, you can now see how space and piece mobility are connected to one another. When analyzing a chess position, it is particularly important to look at all of your opponent's and your own pieces and Pawns. If you notice any of your opponent's pieces have very limited mobility, you may be able to find a way to trap them (take away their only escape routes). What if some of your pieces have limited movement and may be a target for getting trapped? Give them more room! I love trapping Queens—who doesn't?

Quiz 12 *How can Black capture the White Queen in the below diagram? (Note: White's Queen has only two moves: d1 or e2.)*

Answer can be found on page 126.

CONCLUSION

These five advantages/disadvantages should help you devise a plan to target weak Pawns, pieces, or sides of the board and also improve your own position, if needed. If you don't see a straightforward plan to attack your opponent, focus on yourself, and get your pieces to good squares!

10 POWERFUL TACTICS & WHEN TO USE THEM

Tactics

Tactics are short-term plans that involve winning material or achieving checkmate. Easier tactics involve only a couple of moves, but some can include up to 10 moves or even more.

1. Fork

A fork is an attack by a piece on two or more pieces at the same time. We use the general term *fork* a lot, but to be more specific, you can also say "double attack" or "triple attack." A fork can be carried out by any piece in chess, even the King. My personal favorite is the Knight fork!

PAWN FORK

DIAGRAM 7.1:

1. c4+ The Pawn is attacking the King and Rook simultaneously. The King can't capture the Pawn because it is protected by the Rook. The Black King is in check and must move away, which allows the Rook to be captured on the following move. 1. c4+ Kc6; 2. cxb5 Kxb5. White wins 4 points! White captures a Rook, while Black captures only a Pawn.

DIAGRAM 7.1: WHITE
TO MOVE

DIAGRAM 7.2: WHITE TO MOVE

DIAGRAM 7.3: WHITE TO MOVE

DIAGRAM 7.4: BLACK TO MOVE

DIAGRAM 7.2:

1...e5 The Pawn is attacking the Bishop and Knight at the same time. Black won't be able to protect both pieces and must therefore choose to save either the Knight or the Bishop. The Knight and Bishop both have the same value of 3 points, which means it's your choice which to save: (a) 1. e5 Be7; 2. exf6 Bxf6 or (b) 1. e5 Ng4; 2. exd6 cxd6. In both variations, White wins 2 points! White captures a Knight or Bishop, while Black captures only a Pawn.

DIAGRAM 7.3:

1. Nxf7! The Knight is attacking the Queen and Rook at once. The King can't capture the Knight because it is protected by the Bishop. Black must move their Queen, since it is the higher-value piece, but that leaves the Rook to be captured on the following move. 1. Nxf7 Qe7 2. Nxh8. White wins 6 points! White captures the Pawn on f7 and the Rook.

DIAGRAM 7.4:

1...Nd5! The Knight is attacking the King and Queen at the same time, also known as a Royal Fork. The King is in check and must move away, allowing the Queen to be captured on the following move. 1. Nd5+ Kd6 2. Nxb6. Black wins the Queen! Black was already down several points but is able to regain them with the Queen's capture. In the end, Black will be up 5 points (Knight + two Pawns).

BISHOP FORK

DIAGRAM 7.5:

1. Bc6+! The Bishop is attacking the King and Rook simultaneously. The Black King is in check and must move away, which allows the Rook to be captured on the following move. Look out for pieces on the same diagonal! White wins 5 points and captures the Bishop for free.

DIAGRAM 7.6:

1...Bxd4! The Bishop captures the hanging Pawn (unprotected) on d4, which in turn attacks the King and the Knight at the same time. The White King is in check and must move away, which allows the Knight to be captured on the following move. Black captures the Pawn and the Knight and wins 4 points.

ROOK FORK

DIAGRAM 7.7:

1. Rc4+! The Rook is attacking the King and Bishop at the same time. The Black King is in check and must move away, which allows the Bishop to be captured on the following move. White wins 3 points and captures the Bishop for free.

DIAGRAM 7.5: WHITE TO MOVE

DIAGRAM 7.6: BLACK TO MOVE

DIAGRAM 7.7: WHITE TO MOVE

DIAGRAM 7.8: BLACK
TO MOVE

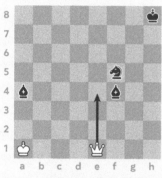

DIAGRAM 7.9: WHITE
TO MOVE

DIAGRAM 7.10: BLACK
TO MOVE

DIAGRAM 7.8:

1...Rd5! The Rook is attacking the Bishop and Knight simultaneously. White can't protect both pieces at once and will have to lose either the Bishop or the Knight. Black wins 3 points and will capture either the Bishop or the Knight for free.

QUEEN FORK

DIAGRAM 7.9:

1. Qe4! The Queen is attacking three pieces at the same time: both Bishops and the Knight! Black won't be able to protect all three at once and will have to lose one of them. White wins 3 points! White will capture either one of the Bishops or the Knight for free.

DIAGRAM 7.10:

1...Qa5+! The Queen is attacking both the King and the Bishop. The White King is in check and must move away or block, which allows the Bishop to be captured on the following move. Black wins 3 points! Black will capture the Bishop for free.

KING FORK

This fork is less popular than the others, but it is still possible. The only problem with the King is that it can never capture a protected piece and usually enters the game only toward the end.

In **DIAGRAM 7.11,** the King is attacking the Knight and the Bishop at the same time. Black won't be able to protect both at once.

ESCAPING A FORK

Protect

If two of your pieces are under attack, see if you can move one to protect the other.

In **DIAGRAM 7.12,** the Black Queen is forking the Rook and Knight, but there's a way to defend both. The Knight moves to d5, where it protects the Rook; the Black Queen can't capture the Knight in this position because it's protected by the Pawn.

Counterattack

A counterattack is the move you make to threaten a higher-ranked piece when your own piece is under attack.

In **DIAGRAM 7.13,** the White Rook is forking the Knight and Bishop, but there are two ways for Black to avoid losing a piece:

1...Bf3+ White must concern themselves with the King, rather than capturing the Knight.

2. Kh2 Ne6 Both the Knight and the Bishop are safe! Another way Black could save the Knight is by protecting it with 1...Be2.

DIAGRAM 7.11: WHITE TO MOVE

DIAGRAM 7.12

DIAGRAM 7.13

DIAGRAM 7.14

Block

In **DIAGRAM 7.14**, White forks the Knight and the King, rather than moving away, while Black comes up with a nice block:

1. . .Be6 The Black Bishop protects the Knight.

2. Bxb3 Bxb3 or **2. Bxe6 Kxe6**

2. Pin

A pin is an attack on a piece that can't or shouldn't move because the King, a higher-value piece, or an unprotected piece is behind it. There are two types of pins in chess: an "absolute pin" and a "relative pin." Not all pins lead to a material advantage. Unlike the fork, the only pieces in chess that can carry out a pin are those that control lines (ranks, files, or diagonals). Which pieces control lines? The Bishop, Rook, and Queen.

ABSOLUTE PIN

An absolute pin is an attack on a piece that *cannot* move because the King is behind it. You can't move a piece under an absolute pin since you're not allowed to put the King into check.

In **DIAGRAM 7.15**, the White Bishop pins the Rook, and it can't move because the King is behind it. Black also can't protect the Rook with any of their own pieces and must lose the Rook at no cost.

DIAGRAM 7.15

In **DIAGRAM 7.16**, the Black Rook is protected by the Bishop and pins the Queen. White has no choice but to lose the Queen: It can't move because of the King behind it. They can either play 1. Qxa5 or wait to be captured; either way, Black wins the Queen for a Rook.

DIAGRAM 7.16

RELATIVE PIN

A relative pin is an attack on a piece that shouldn't move because there is a higher-value or unprotected piece behind it. The reason I'm saying the piece *shouldn't* move (instead of *can't*) is that you can still move that piece; it just wouldn't be a good move and might result in loss of material.

ATTACKING THE PINNED PIECE

Not all pins lead to a material advantage, but if you attack the pinned piece, it's a different story.

In **DIAGRAM 7.17**, the Black Knight on c6 is pinned by the Bishop, so capturing it would just lead to a trade.

1. d5! This move wins the Knight since it's under an absolute pin: The King is behind it.

2. ..0-0

3. dxc6 The Black Knight is pinned by the Queen and Rook, but White can't capture it because the Knight is protected. (See **DIAGRAM 7.18**.)

DIAGRAM 7.17

DIAGRAM 7.18

1. f4! If the Knight moves, it will allow White to capture the Queen.

2. . .Nc6 Black can also ignore this but will get captured on the next move: 1. . .Qe7 (trying to get out of the pin); 2. fxe5 wins the Knight for a Pawn. This option is better for Black.

3. Qxe7 Nxe7

4. Rxe7

White wins the Knight!

IMMOBILIZED PIECE

Whatever the pinned piece was protecting before, it no longer does until getting out of the pin.

In **DIAGRAM 7.19**, the Knight on c6 is under an absolute pin by the Bishop, which means it no longer defends the e5 Pawn. White can simply play 1. Bxe5 here and win a free Pawn!

In **DIAGRAM 7.20**, the White Pawn on d4 is pinned by the Rook (the Queen is behind), which means the Knight is no longer protected:

1. . .Bxc5!

2. dxc5?? Rxd2

White shouldn't capture the Bishop, because they will lose their Queen for a Rook. A better move would be to try to get out of the 2. Qe3.

DIAGRAM 7.19

DIAGRAM 7.20

GETTING OUT OF THE PIN

Try attacking the piece that's pinning yours!

In **DIAGRAM 7.21**, Black's Knight is under attack and can't move—if they do nothing to stop this, their Knight will be captured on the next move:

1. ..a6 Black attacks the Bishop in return.

2. Ba4 b5 White is trying to keep the pin on the Knight (hoping to still win it), but Black destroys their plan by playing b5. If White plays 2. Bxc6 bxc6; 3. dxc6, they win a Pawn but not the Knight. If White plays 2. dxc6 axb5; 3. cxb7 Bxb7; 4. Nxb5, they are also up a Pawn but still don't gain the Knight.

3. Bb3 Na5

Maybe this wasn't the best example, since Black loses some material either way, but it's definitely preferable to lose a Pawn than a Knight!

DIAGRAM 7.21

3. Skewer

A skewer is an attack on a piece that forces it to move and allows you to capture a higher-value or unprotected piece behind it.

In **DIAGRAM 7.22**, White's King and Rook are on the same line:

1. ..Rad8 (or Rfd8) The King is in check and must move away.

2. Ke5 Rxd1 Black wins a Rook! Black's King and Rook are on the same diagonal.

DIAGRAM 7.22

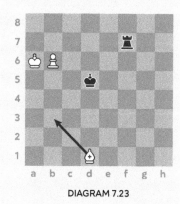

DIAGRAM 7.23

DIAGRAM 7.24

DIAGRAM 7.25

DIAGRAM 7.23:

1. Bb3+ Kd4 The King must get out of check.

DIAGRAM 7.24:

2. Bxf7 White wins the Rook and, shortly, the game. White's King and Queen are on the same diagonal.

1. . .Qf5+ The King can't capture the protected Queen and must run away.

2. Ke3 Qxb1 Black wins the Queen!

In **DIAGRAM 7.25**, Black's Bishop and Knight are on the same line. This example is interesting because it's a pin and skewer at the same time.

1. Ra4 Bd6 If 1. . .Ne3 2. Rxb4, White wins either the Bishop or the Knight!

ESCAPING THE SKEWER

Protect

When your piece is under attack, you can move it to a square where it protects the piece behind it.

In **DIAGRAM 7.26**, both of Black's Knights are on the d file, and one of the Knights is currently under attack by the Rook. If Black makes an incorrect move here, they will lose material.

If Black chooses **1. . .N2c4** or **1. . .N6c4**, the Knights end up protecting each other.

Block

In **DIAGRAM 7.27**, Black was threatening the Queen and hoping it would move aside so the Bishop could capture the Rook. Instead, White finds a way to protect against the threat and block the Bishop's diagonal.

Counterplay

In **DIAGRAM 7.28**, Black's Queen is under attack; if it moves to an incorrect square, the Bishop will capture the Rook:

1. ..Qf5+! White must be concerned about their King.

2. Ka1 Rc8 Black's Queen and Rook are safe.

4. Discovered Check/Attack

Discovered check and attack is when a player moves one piece but then switches to a different piece to make the actual attack. I like to call this tactic a "surprise attack." There are many cases when this tactic looks very much like a double attack (fork), so it's important to understand the difference: A fork is when a piece attacks two or more at the same time, while a discovered attack can be two pieces attacking two or more at once.

DIAGRAM 7.26

DIAGRAM 7.27

DIAGRAM 7.28

DIAGRAM 7.29

DIAGRAM 7.30

DIAGRAM 7.31

DISCOVERED CHECK

A discovered check is a surprise attack that includes checking the King.

In **DIAGRAM 7.29**, the White Queen wants to check the King, but the Knight is in the way. The Knight moves to c6, and now Black's King and Queen are under attack simultaneously. The Knight is attacking the Queen, and the King is checked by the Queen, so Black will have to lose their Queen for a Knight:

1. Nc6++ Be7

2. Nxd8

DISCOVERED ATTACK

Discovered attack is a surprise attack that doesn't include checking the King—just other pieces.

In **DIAGRAM 7.30**, White moves the Knight to attack the Rook; the Bishop simultaneously attacks the other Rook. Black won't be able to move both at the same time, so sadly, they must lose a Rook for either a Knight or a Bishop.

DIAGRAM 7.31 is an interesting example that requires a capture. Black notices that the Rook is an unprotected piece and on the same diagonal as the Queen:

1. . .Nxe4

2. fxe4 Bxa1

Black gives up the Knight but captures a Pawn and Rook in return. White could have also responded with **2. Qd1 Bxa1; 3. Qxa1 Nxg3; 4. hxg3**—winning for Black.

5. Double Check

Double check is one of the strongest tactics in chess. This one is pretty self-explanatory: It's when the King is being checked by two pieces at the same time. It's not possible to have triple check in chess. If you have three or more pieces attacking the King, then one of the pieces must have already been attacking the King in previous moves.

Why is double check a very strong move? Because in this case, the ABCs of check do not apply. The King's only way out of check is to run away. If you put your opponent under a double check, they won't be able to block or capture. Most double checks lead to winning of material or checkmate.

1. . .Bb4# Black is checking the King with the Bishop and Queen simultaneously, which means no block or capture is possible. The King simply has no escape routes. Checkmate! (See **DIAGRAM 7.32**.)

1. Nf6++ Kf8 Double check by the Knight and Bishop—the King must move to a safe square. (See **DIAGRAM 7.33**.)

2. Re8#

1. Bg5+ Kc7 Double check: The King must move! If Black moves, 1. . .Ke8; 2. Rd8#. (See **DIAGRAM 7.34**.)

2. Bd8#

NOTE: You can't escape from double check. If this happens, you have to move your King—there's no other option!

DIAGRAM 7.32

DIAGRAM 7.33

DIAGRAM 7.34

DIAGRAM 7.35

DIAGRAM 7.36

DIAGRAM 7.37

6. Removing the Defender

If your opponent's piece is protecting another piece or planning a threat, you should try to get rid of it.

In **DIAGRAM 7.35**, Black's Rook and Knight protect against the back-rank checkmate. Let's get those obstacles out of the way!

1. Rxc8 Nxc8 This eliminates the Rook, Black capturing it with the Knight. This opens up the d file for White's Rook.

2. Rd8# Black is putting pressure on the g2 Pawn. If the White Knight weren't on f4, Black would checkmate: Qxg2. Let's see if we can remove the defender. (See **DIAGRAM 7.36**.)

1. ..g5

2. f3 gxf4 Alternative move: **2. Nd3 Qxg2#**.

In **DIAGRAM 7.37**, the Black Rook is putting pressure on the Bishop, whose only protector is the Knight. Can we get rid of it? YES!

1. ..Bxg3 It's up to White here if they want to save the Bishop or the Knight—either way they lose one. If White wants to save the Bishop, they will play 2. Bf3 Bb8, and Black will be up one Knight.

2. fxg3 Rxe5

7. Sacrifices

SACRIFICING FOR CHECKMATE

If the White Rook weren't on the 1st rank in **DIAGRAM 7.38**, Black would be able to checkmate with Re1! We must remove it to prolong our plans.

1. ..Qxd1 Who cares about the Queen when there's checkmate?

2. Nxd1 Re1#

DIAGRAM 7.38

SACRIFICING FOR MATERIAL ADVANTAGE

DIAGRAM 7.39:

1. Qxh8+!! Kxh8 Why on earth would White give up their Queen for the Rook?

2. Nxf7+ Kg7 White wins back the Queen using a royal fork!

3. Nxd6 White sacrifices their Queen but retrieves the Rook, the Pawn, and the Queen. Beautiful tactic! White is threatening to win the game by playing 1. Qg5+ and then 2. Qg7#, so Black has to act fast. Black notices that White's pieces are lined up on the 5th rank.

DIAGRAM 7.39

DIAGRAM 7.40

DIAGRAM 7.41

DIAGRAM 7.42

1. Qxd5!! Kxd5 Another Queen sacrifice—really? (See **DIAGRAM 7.40**.)

2. Rb5 Black wins back the Queen and increases material. Black gains a significant advantage because they give up their Queen (–9 points) but get a Knight and the Queen (+12 points) in return.

8. Decoy

The decoy is a tactic that draws the King or Queen onto a square or line where it didn't intend to move. Sacrifices are very common.

Black's attack in **DIAGRAM 7.41** is very strong. Black's Knight, Rook, and Queen are looking toward the King:

1. . .Rxf1 This move looks like a trade—and, in this case, it is—but Black wants to push the King to the f1 square.

2. Kxf1 Qf2#

1. d5! Qxd5?? White is trying to force the Black Queen onto the d file. White's best move is to not capture the Pawn, move away from the Queen, and give up the Knight. Giving up the Knight is better than losing the Queen. (See **DIAGRAM 7.42**.)

2. Bxh7+ Kxh7 Using a discovered attack of the Rook, Black's best move is to capture the Bishop, since they'd at least get something in return for the loss of their Queen.

3. Rxd5 White wins the Queen for a Bishop!

In **DIAGRAM 7.43**, Black's King isn't very safe here—but is only one move from castling. White notices that if the Queen weren't on c6, the Knight could achieve a fork by playing Nc7+.

1. Bb5 Qxb5 The Queen is under an absolute pin! Black decides to capture the Bishop and goes into a royal fork.

2. Nc7+ White gives up their Bishop to gain the Queen. Success!

DIAGRAM 7.43

9. Deflection

Deflection is the act of forcing an opponent's piece to give up protecting a square or other piece.

In **DIAGRAM 7.44**, White's Queen is putting pressure on Black's Queen. Seeing that the only defender of the Black Queen is the King, White thinks, "Let's get the King to stop protecting the Queen!"

1. Re8!! Kxe8

2. Qxg7 White wins the Queen for a Rook.

The Black Queen in **DIAGRAM 7.45** is putting pressure on White's Queen, and the only defender is the Rook on d1. This example also demonstrates the case of an overloaded piece (see page 115). The Rook on d1 is overloaded because it's busy protecting against back-rank checkmate and the Queen. Sadly, that's too much for the Rook to handle.

DIAGRAM 7.44

DIAGRAM 7.45

DIAGRAM 7.46

1. ..Re1+ White must capture the Rook to prevent checkmate but, in the process, loses their Queen.

2. Rxe1 Qxd4 Black wins the Queen for the Rook.

The move in **DIAGRAM 7.46** is one I find more complicated than the previous examples, because you don't expect players to underpromote in chess.

The White King is protecting the Rook in danger, so instead of capturing it right away, Black wants the King to stop protecting the Rook.

1. ..Qh2+

2. Kxh2 gxf1=N

The King must capture the Queen; otherwise 2. Kf2 gxf1=Q, 3. Kxf1 Qxd2, and Black will gain a Queen. After the King captures the Queen, Black captures the Rook and promotes the Pawn into a Knight to execute a royal fork against the White Queen and King.

3. Kg2 Nxd2

In the end, Black is 2 points ahead.

10. Overloaded Pieces

An overloaded piece is one that is responsible for too many defensive duties, so at some point it won't be able to manage them all. In **DIAGRAM 7.47**, Black's Pawn on d7 is overloaded because it's protecting both the Bishop and Knight:

1. Rxc6 dxc6

2. Rxe6 White obtains a Bishop and Knight for a Rook. A Knight and Bishop are preferable to a Rook because of their point value: The Knight and Bishop equal 6 points (3 + 3 = 6 points), while the Rook equals 5 points.

In **DIAGRAM 7.48**, White's Rook on b1 is overloaded: It's protecting against the Queen's check and also checkmate, Rf1#.

1. ..Qb6+!! White can't capture the Queen or else there will be checkmate: 2. Rf1#.

2. Be3 Qxb1+ Black accepts the free Rook.

3. Rd1 Qb2 Black has won the Rook as well as gaining a superior attacking position.

In **DIAGRAM 7.49**, Black's Knight is overloaded: It's protecting the Bishop on d5 as well as the checkmate square, Qh7#.

1. Rxd5! Nxd5?? The best move for Black is to play 1...g6. Then White will reply by moving their Rook away to a safe square.

2. Qh7#

DIAGRAM 7.47

DIAGRAM 7.48

DIAGRAM 7.49

Tactic puzzles.

1. White to move and find the fork.

2. Black to move and find the skewer.

3. White to move and find the double check.

4. Black to move and find the absolute pin.

5. White to move and find the defender.

6. Black to move and find the fork.

7. White to move and find the discovered attack.

8. Black to move and find the sacrifice.

9. White to move and find the discovered check.

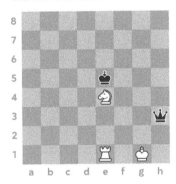

Answers can be found on page 127.

WHAT'S NEXT?

You've made it! Congratulations!

How do you feel? Has your confidence grown?

If you're a little stuck on certain concepts, I highly recommend reading the book again—paying special attention to the more complex diagrams. Don't be embarrassed to read it a few times, since everyone absorbs information at a different pace. There's a lot of information to take in, but that's chess—it's one of the most complicated board games of all time. I hope this book has given you a basic understanding of the rules and some of the fundamental concepts of tactics and strategies.

As a chess instructor, I've tried to put in writing here as much of my knowledge as possible in a concise, practical format—and in limited space. (If I were to write a detailed book on all possible aspects of chess, on the other hand, it'd be more than 100,000 pages.) Keep in mind that reading this book alone is not enough to become a good chess player; you must read others, as well—especially on specialized topics. When I was a child, I mostly read books on strategy, tactics, endgame, and analysis of grandmaster games. I was never interested in opening theory, since it's very repetitive. The more you play, you will find some topics more interesting to you than others.

Playing

Playing the game is key, of course. How can you get good at something without practicing?

OVER-THE-BOARD GAMES

Make an effort to write down your moves! Most competitive tournaments will force you to do so, for the purpose of proving draws. If you have the moves written down, you can go home and analyze the game afterward. Most beginner players can't remember all the moves of a game—this comes only with practice.

Another suggestion is to ask your opponent after your game whether or not they'd like to go over the game together. I used to do this, regardless of whether I won or lost, because I was always curious to find out what my opponent was thinking during the game. If you lost, I definitely suggest going over the game with your opponent. If you're playing against someone without writing your moves down, and you lose, make sure to ask what mistakes you made and what you could have done better. Your opponent can give you some insight. Some players will oblige; some won't. Just take a chance and ask—you never know!

ONLINE GAMES

Online games are the most convenient way to play at home or whenever you're on the go. One huge benefit is that you don't have to write down moves—the app or website does it for you. After each game, make sure to analyze the game with a computer engine. Check out Lichess.org's analysis feature—I recommend it to all my students. One problem with online chess is that, sadly, there are a lot of cheaters. If you are aware of a suspicious player, make sure to notify the website. Cheating is a problem in all sports, and we need to fully banish it, but as long as most of us stay truthful, the beauty of the game continues.

"You win or you learn." Another favorite quote! Don't pout when you lose or see your mistakes. Imagine if you always won—that would mean you were not playing against sufficiently challenging players. If you keep playing against the same opponents and beating them, you won't improve. Instead, think about rising up one level of opponent—you might lose against the stronger players at first, but eventually you will get to their level with practice and study.

Studying

Studying involves reading books, solving puzzles, participating in chess discussions, and a lot more. The benefit of the Internet is that you can find all types of learning materials, both for purchase and free. When my father was coaching me, I'd create a schedule to study chess almost every day for one to two hours. It's a good idea to read chess books, even a few at the same time, but make sure not to read several in one day. If you decide to read a strategy book that day, stick to that one for the day and switch to a tactics book tomorrow. You want your mind to process as much information as possible without getting confused. Puzzles are never bad, either—you can do them every day! Other chess instructors have different methods, so do whatever floats your boat.

BALANCE

It's important to maintain a good balance between studying and playing. Playing too much and not increasing your knowledge in other aspects of the game can lead to very slow improvement—unless you analyze every game! At the same time, studying but not playing (or playing very little) doesn't make sense, either, because you've got to make sure what you've read in books can be implemented into the game.

Reaching Out to Compete

"A computer once beat me at chess,
but it was no match for me at kickboxing."
—Emo Philips

CLUBS AND TOURNAMENTS

Check out your nearest chess club! If you've never been to a chess club or tournament, I would suggest finding a casual, social one in the beginning. At first, competitive chess clubs and tournaments can seem intimidating, because everyone must be quiet to not bother surrounding players. I run Pub Chess Toronto, a social chess club located in the downtown area of the city. It's divided into a casual playing section and a tournament section, but no one minds if people talk. Chess clubs usually offer casual games (no timer and unrated) or tournament games (with timer and rated/unrated). It's up to you to decide which one you're ready for, but make sure to eventually try out a tournament.

QUIZ ANSWERS

Chapter Five

1. Checkmate. The King is in check and no ABCs are possible.

2. Stalemate. The King is not in check and no legal moves or captures are possible.

3. Check. The Queen can be captured: Kxh8.

4. Check. The Bishop can block: Bc8.

5. Check. The King can still move: Kd7.

6. Checkmate. The King is in check and no ABCs are possible.

7. Stalemate. The King is not in check and no legal moves or captures are possible.

8. Stalemate. The King is not in check and no legal moves or captures are possible.

9. Check. The Queen can capture: Qxa8.

Chapter Six

1. White's Knight and a4 Pawn. Both are not controlling the center. Remember this about the Knight: "The Knight on the rim is dim."

2. **1. Nxh5** White wins 3 points.

    Incorrect answers:

    a) 1. Rxa4 leads to trade of Rooks.

    b) 1. Rxd6?? This would give up the Rook for a Pawn, losing 4 points.

    c) 1. Rxh4?? This would give up a Rook for a Knight, losing 2 points.

    1...Qxg5 Black wins 3 points.

    Incorrect answers:

    a) 1...cxd5 leads to a Pawn trade.

    b) 1...Bxc3 leads to a Bishop-Knight trade.

    c) 1...fxg3 leads to another Pawn trade.

3. White is attacking the h8 Rook. Black has two responses: **1...Nf6** or **1...f6.**

    Incorrect answers:

    a) 1...e5?; 2. Bxe5. White wins the Pawn and continues the attack on the Rook.

    b) 1...Bg7??; 2. Bxg7. White wins the Bishop and continues attacking the Rook.

4. **1...Rxe2** When White moved their Bishop, they stopped protecting the e2 Pawn.

5. **1...Qe7** or **1...Qf6** When White played 1. d4, the intent wasn't only to get the Pawn into the center, but also to open up the c1 Bishop, which happens to be attacking the Queen.

    Incorrect answer: 1...exd4??; 2. Bxg5

6. **1. Bf1**

    Incorrect answer: 1. Re1?? Rxe1 loses the Rook.

    1. Kg2

    Incorrect answer: 1. Re1?? Rxe1 loses the Rook.

7. **1. Qf3**

8. Yes! It wouldn't be good for Black to play **1...Qxf7??; 2. Bxf7 Kxf7**. White will win a Queen and Pawn, while Black gets the Knight and Bishop. Black will lose 4 points.

9. Black has 23 points on the board, while White has 15 points on the board. Black has 8 more points.

10. White's c2 and c3 Pawns are doubled. White's g2, g4, and g5 Pawns are tripled. Black's b6 and b7 Pawns are doubled.

11. Isolated pawns can be problematic, because they can't be protected by other Pawns and must use higher-value pieces as protection. The higher-value pieces could be more useful elsewhere, rather than babysitting a Pawn.

12. **1...Bg4!** Queen is trapped! The h3 Pawn can't capture the Bishop because it is under an absolute pin. If the Queen captures the Bishop, the g6 Rook will capture the Queen.

Chapter Seven

1. **1. Bd5**

2. **1...a1=Q**

3. **1. Nf7# or 1. Ng6#**

4. **1...Rc4**

5. **1. Bxc6 bxc6 2. Rxe4** (1. Rxe4 also works since the Bishop is under an absolute pin.)

6. **1...d4**

7. **1. Nd5 Qa4 2. Nxc7+**

8. **1...Rxh2 2. Kxh2 Qh4#**

9. **1. Nf2+ or 1. Ng5+**

RESOURCES

WEBSITES

Most chess websites are fairly similar, presenting learning materials, articles, puzzles, news, tournament coverage, and more. Below, I highlight a few features that make these sites notable and unique.

Chess.com The top chess website with over a million users, this very well-funded site offers three different memberships, depending on your needs. Many functions are free but have limited use. For example, there's a specified number of chess puzzles you can access per day, unless you purchase a membership.

Chessbase.com The top website for chess news.

Chessgames.com One of the biggest databases of players' games all over the world.

Chess24.com Another top chess site for general use that competes with Chess.com.

Chesstempo.com The best chess site for puzzles! This website offers chess puzzles of every kind.

Lichess.org A free website that has gained recent popularity. Lichess has an amazing tool that analyzes the games you've played with a computer engine to tell you how many mistakes you and your opponent have made. With every mistake, the engine tests you on what you or your opponent could have done better, rather than giving you the answer right away.

BOOKS

Winning Chess series, by Yasser Seirawan: An outstanding series of books by a top-ranked U.S. player and chess commentator. Titles in the series include: *Winning Chess Tactics, Winning Chess Strategies, Winning Chess Openings,* and others.

MOVIES

Magnus Biography of Magnus Carlsen, current and second-youngest World Champion.

Pawn Sacrifice Biography of Bobby Fischer and his important win over World Champion Boris Spassky. Tobey Maguire portrays Fischer.

Queen of Katwe A beautiful movie that tells the story of a young, dedicated girl (Fiona) from Uganda, who was able to become a strong chess player with the help of her community.

Searching for Bobby Fischer The story of a young boy who is passionate about chess, gets noticed for his talent, and later becomes a prodigy with the help of his trainer.

STREAMERS

Anna Rudolf A talented chess player who annotates while she plays. Anna does a lot of collaborative streams with other chess players. A very popular lady.

Chessbrahs A team of Canadian chess players who entertain online while playing. All are highly qualified chess masters who commentate during important tournaments/events.

CHESS HISTORY

"Bobby Fischer." *Wikipedia*. Last modified September 4, 2018.
https://en.wikipedia.org/wiki/Bobby_Fischer.

"Deep Blue versus Garry Kasparov." *Wikipedia*. Last modified August 16, 2018.
https://en.wikipedia.org/wiki/Deep_Blue_versus_Garry_Kasparov.

"Garry Kasparov." *Wikipedia*. Last modified August 29, 2018.
https://en.wikipedia.org/wiki/Garry_Kasparov.

"History of Chess." *Wikipedia*. Last modified August 12, 2018.
https://simple.wikipedia.org/wiki/History_of_chess.

"Judit Polgár." *Wikipedia*. Last modified August 25, 2018.
https://en.wikipedia.org/wiki/Judit_Polgár.

"Magnus Carlsen." *Wikipedia*. Last modified September 2, 2018.
https://en.wikipedia.org/wiki/Magnus_Carlsen.

"Timur Gareyev Breaks Blindfold Record." *Chess News*. December 5, 2016.
https://en.chessbase.com/post/timur-gareyev-world-record-blindfold-attempt.

GLOSSARY

50-MOVE RULE: If a Pawn hasn't been moved or a piece hasn't been captured in 50 moves, either player may claim a draw.

ABSOLUTE PIN: An attack on a piece that can't move because the King is behind it.

CASTLE/CASTLING: A special move that puts your King into safety, consisting of moving the King two squares toward an unmoved Rook and moving the Rook to the other side of the King.

CHECK: When the King is under attack but can escape by running away, blocking, and/or capturing the attacking piece.

CHECKMATE: When the King is under attack but can't escape by running away, blocking, and/or capturing the attacking piece. This scenario ends a chess game.

CLOSED POSITION: A position that has mostly blocked files and diagonals.

COUNTERATTACK: Responding to an attack on your pawn by attacking one of your opponent's pawns of the same or higher value.

DECOY: A tactic that involves drawing the King or Queen to a square or line where they don't want to go.

DEFENDER: A piece that protects a piece or square, or protects against a threat.

DEFLECTION: The act of forcing your opponent's piece to give up protecting a square or another piece.

DEVELOP: To move pieces from their starting position to new locations where they control a greater number of squares and have greater mobility.

DISCOVERED ATTACK: When you move a piece to open the way for another piece to make an attack.

DISCOVERED CHECK: When you move a piece to open the way for another piece to attack the King.

DOUBLE CHECK: When the King is under attack by two pieces simultaneously.

DOUBLE/TRIPLE PAWNS: When two or three Pawns (of the same color) are on the same file.

FIANCHETTO BISHOP: When you develop your Bishop on the longest diagonal (either a1 to h8 or a8 to h1) and hide in a fortress of Pawns.

FILES: Vertical lines that consist of eight squares, lettered along a chessboard: a, b, c, d, e, f, g, and h files. In non-chess contexts, we call them columns.

FLEEING SQUARE: Escape square for the King.

FORK: An attack on a piece or Pawn by two or more pieces at the same time. Also known as double attack, triple attack, and so on.

HANGING PIECE: An unprotected piece.

INSUFFICIENT MATERIAL: When neither side has enough pieces to checkmate the other's King.

ISOLATED PAWNS: Pawns that can't be protected by other Pawns.

KINGSIDE: The half of the board that consists of the e, f, g, and h files.

MATERIAL: All the pieces.

OPENING: A series of moves in the beginning of the game.

OPEN POSITION: A position that has mostly open or semi-open files and diagonals.

OVERLOADED PIECE: A piece that is responsible for too many defensive duties and at some point won't be able to manage them all.

PASSED PAWN: A Pawn that can't be stopped by opposing Pawns but can be by other pieces.

PAWN BASE: The Pawn that starts the pawn chain.

PAWN CHAIN: Pawns that are linked together by protecting one another. Pawn chains are positioned on a diagonal.

PAWN ISLANDS: A group of Pawns connected by files.

PERPETUAL CHECK: When you check the King repeatedly and are able to copy the exact same position three times.

PROMOTION: A Pawn's ability, when it reaches the other side of the board, to turn itself into a Queen, Rook, Knight, or Bishop.

QUEENSIDE: The half of the board that consists of the a, b, c, and d files.

RANKS: Horizontal lines that consist of eight squares, numbered along a chessboard: 1st, 2nd, 3rd, 4th, 5th, 6th, 7th, and 8th ranks. In non-chess contexts, we call them rows.

RELATIVE PIN: An attack on a piece that shouldn't move because there is a higher-value or unprotected piece behind it.

SKEWER: An attack on a lower-value piece with the goal of also capturing the higher-value or unprotected piece behind it.

SMOTHERED MATE: When the King is in check and can't escape because it is trapped by its own pieces.

STALEMATE: When the King is not in check but no legal moves can be made by either side.

TEMPO: Time, in the form of a turn. When you gain a tempo, you gain more time. Losing a tempo is lost time.

THREE-TIME REPETITION: Copying the exact same position three times but without checks.

VARIANTS: The different moves that can be played after the starting moves.

INDEX

ABOUT THE AUTHOR

YELIZAVETA ORLOVA is a nationally ranked player who represented Canada numerous times at the World Youth Chess Championship and World Chess Olympiad. An experienced coach for over seven years, she hopes to be a chess writer.

CPSIA information can be obtained
at www.ICGtesting.com
Printed in the USA
BVHW050616030119
536790BV00001B/2